also from
clearing skies press

Keeping the Baby Alive till Your Wife Gets Home

Keeping Your Toddler on Track till Mommy Gets Back

Keeping Your Grandkids Alive till Their Ungrateful Parents Arrive: The Guide for Fun-Loving Granddads

. . . .

upcoming from
clearing skies press

Keeping the Baby Alive till Your Wife Gets Home
Deluxe Edition

The Budget-Romance Traveler: Real *Florida*

Cover design by Ed Cahill

Distributed by Independent Publishers Group

Motherhood EXPOSED

Surviving Myth Conceptions
of Postmodern Parenting...
through Good Times and Bad

Dear Ed,
I can't thank you
enough
for the
smart design
decisions you made
for this book.
Your friend,
Skeet

KATHERINE GRACE

clearing skies press

a clearing skies press original, First Edition. April, 2005.

Clearing Skies Press 4002 Dunbarton Way Roswell, GA 30075
770-518-8931 visit us @ clearingskies.com

ISBN 0-9707937-5-8

Printed in the United States of America.

Publisher's Cataloging-in-Publication Data:

Grace, Katherine.
Motherhood Exposed : surviving myth conceptions of postmodern parenting...through good times and bad / by Katherine Grace.
--1st ed.
p. cm.

1. Motherhood 2. Parenting. 3. Parenting Humor.
4. Mother and Child. I. Title

HQ759.9.G62 2005 306.874'5—dc22

10 9 8 7 6 5 4 3 2 1

Despite every effort to furnish the reader with precise, authoritative, indispensible information, the publisher and author accept no responsibility whatever for any myth bursting which occurs during routine motherhood duty. Children who disagree with the content herein may lodge complaints only after reaching adulthood and attaining financial independence.

Dedicated

to David—who believed

Table of Contents

It's Time to Clear the Air

an introduction

We all set out to make something of our lives. We have professional goals we set, dreams to achieve, degrees to be gotten...with motherhood it is no different.

We dream about how our children will some day think of us as the best mother who ever lived. We will be able to be flexible, and yet set boundaries, always be understanding and yet firm, forever project a playful, yet serious temperament. We will be smart enough to help our kids with algebraic equations, yet in touch enough to not seem too corny or out of date.

We will be respected and yet never feared. We will be able to convey years' worth of trial-and-error parenting education so we can save our own children from the same misfortunes. Meanwhile, we will not repeat the mistakes of our parents.

Somewhere between these dreams and reality, children are born, and when the smoke clears what rises from the ashes is a myth.

Over the past thirteen years of motherhood, I have encountered many issues that, in a prior life, I thought I would handle differently. I have witnessed events that I assumed I was well equipped for, only to find a thirteen-year-old standing in front of me looking at me like I have no idea what I'm talking about. Over the years I have been reduced from an intelligent woman with thoughts and opinions, into a robot who can successfully fill a sippie cup with apple juice while sorting laundry with the other hand. From someone who left the house well groomed, to a woman who has become an out of date fashion nightmare who can't find her make-up bag, much less find time to put some on.

Basically, I have gone from someone who felt capable in most capacities, to a mom (according to my children) who wears stupid clothes, listens to stupid music, has stupid opinions, and establishes exceptionally stupid rules.

Reflecting on this evolution reminds me of a friend who recently married and came over to tell me the good news. She and her husband were ready to have a baby. She started listing to me all of the plans she had for her child...

"See, John and I are going to establish boundaries early.

I think if a child knows the rules immediately, he or she will form lifelong habits."

I laughed.

"Better just hide anything that's valuable now, and save yourself the trouble."

"No, you see, you and your husband let the kids run the show. You stay home on weekends. You're always driving someone somewhere. Your house is full of screaming kids all the time. It's not that I'm saying you're doing it wrong or anything; it's just that John and I have decided to handle things differently.

"We're not going to hide our expensive knick-knacks. We're going to teach them how to respect Mom and Dad's property. We're going to explain to them when they're older that we too have a life, and that they need to work around us if necessary."

I again laughed heartily, wished my friend the best of luck, and advised her to consider adopting a pet instead.

She gave me the look that told me she didn't understand, and would never understand until she had children of her own.

And so out of the need to dispel some of the existing myths of parenting, I set out to write from my own experiences. With what little brain power I have present, and some of the tongue left in my cheek, I give you this book. If you too feel that having children will not change your lives unless you let it, if you hold to the belief that a child raised right will not falter from the path the parent has laid out for him or her, perhaps it's time to sift through the charred embers of myth-making and embrace the true realities of motherhood.

Certainly the things you teach your children matter. Certainly rules you establish, and morals you instill make a difference. But in the end parenting is an art and definitely not a science. What works for you today, will most likely not work tomorrow, and just when you think you can finally get around to taking your Christmas card picture, your oldest daughter will dye her hair blue, regret it, and you won't be able to get her out of her room for 48 hours.

There is only so much you can control until the day your child informs you she has her own mind and she's not afraid to use it, thank you very much, Mom.

Have I lost my sense of self-worth in this slow and sometimes painful transformation into enlightened motherhood? I would like to think that instead of losing all sanity, I have gained a sense of humor. Do I have all the answers? Of course not! Will children change your lives? Definitely! Would you trade them for anything in the world? Never.

And so, for parents everywhere who have cleared their own smoke, and come to embrace their temporary lack of intelligence, and for prospective parents who have yet to discover how little they know, I hope you warm to a few of the heartfelt insights which follow...

Surviving Myth Conceptions of Postmodern Parenting...
through Good Times and Bad

Motherhood EXPOSED

Katherine Grace

Myth:
I Will Maintain My Sanity in Spite of My Children

Chapter one

How My Mind Works

I am a thinker. Don't get me wrong, I am not categorizing myself as a deep-thinker like Plato or Aristotle. I am just a consistently analytical thinker, which translated to human terms means, that under any and all circumstances, I think too much. Back when you were in school, this was an asset. However, when you become a mother this talent becomes less than a positive attribute.

Example: the other day my 13-year-old daughter asked me where the bread is. I am of the understanding that "normal" people probably would just say something simple, to the effect of, "It's on top of the fridge." I am not normal people.

After 13 years of raising children something bizarre has happened to my thought process, so instead of answering right away, I begin thinking in my head thoughts that approximate this:

You have lived here how long, and you still don't know where we keep the bread? Is it too much trouble to actually look first before you claim you can't find something? Then again, I don't always put the bread on top of the fridge. Sometimes it's on the counter or on top of the microwave. But wait a minute, is that too much to ask? That you check three whole places? I mean our kitchen is very small; it's not like I hide the bread or anything. It's right out in the open. It's not secret stealth bread. It's not on an underground mission to hide itself. Although, nobody in this house ever puts anything back where it belongs, so maybe it is missing somehow?

Now I need to clarify. During this mental conversation taking place in my head, my daughter is not standing there for hours staring at me. This all occurs in the space of a few seconds. What I turned to my daughter and said however was very different....

"I'm not sure."

That's what I said.

"I'm not sure."

* * *

Now don't mistake this statement for one of ultimate self-control or anything (although I have those moments too, as any Mom will tell you). This is a statement of confusion. I have thought so much, in such a short period of time, that I have bewildered myself. I no longer care about bread; I am now simply trying to figure out why I thought those things.

Why are you so upset over a loaf of bread? All she did was walk in from school and ask for bread. What kind of a person freaks out over bread? It's like yelling over spilled milk. It's an accident. You can't get upset over a silly accident. But wait a minute. This was no accident. She deliberately didn't even look for the bread. I mean how long has she lived here?

And thus, the cycle starts over. I look at my daughter, who has decided that the bread was too hard to find, and has opted for a bowl of ice cream instead.

Oh, the therapy this child is going to need if I keep this up, I think to myself.

But wait a minute, I didn't say any of this out loud, so she'll be just fine. Of course, I'm raising a child who can't find bread, in her own kitchen, in a house she's lived in for how long?

The debate rages. Am I raising children who will never be able cope in the modern world, or do I worry needlessly about trivial incidents regarding their behavior? When you really break it down, what is reality? Which is more important, being a good mother or maintaining your sanity? Are the two qualities incompatible?

Come to think of it, I think she might not be the one with the huge therapy bills....

Myth:

No Means No

Chapter two

The Birds

I have birds in my house. Parakeets to be more precise. Three of them. Purchased on one of those occasions when I actually bought into false promises from my three children.

"Of course we'll take care of them, Mom. We'll feed them every day, and clean them every week, and play with them all the time and...."

You get the idea.

Anyone who has children, knows this speech, and likewise, knows better than to buy into it. Or to take any child into a pet store in the first place. I took them there and I bought into their sales pitch. No question about it, the birds are my fault.

Please don't get me wrong. I love animals. I love zoos. I love aquariums. I am all for animal rights. Just not in my own home, at three in the morning, when I awake to screeching that rivals any horror movie soundtrack. For those of you who don't know better, birds are not quiet animals. They do not know the difference between day and night, and the tiniest speck of light sends them into a chirping festival.

Now, my kids have a tendency to leave the bathroom light on in the middle of the night, which of course makes the birds assume that it must be daytime. And until I provide substantial proof that it is otherwise, the birds won't be quiet. Which basically means that I have to get up and turn off the light. Needless to say, this has not made me extremely fond of the birds.

Another problem with adding them to our family is that all the guarantees about feeding and watering them flew out the window the first week after the birds came home.

The first week after their arrival in our house was like watching a bad *Brady Bunch* re-run. My youngest didn't want to go to school because her bird would miss her. My oldest informed me that she was going to save up her allowance to buy her bird its own cage, so it could live in her room. My middle one started using our upstairs bathtub as a bird "playland" of sorts.

No day was complete without the birds coming out and being played with. Every child in our neighborhood was invited over to see the birds. The birds even started to look a little on the heavy side, since secretly every single child was feeding them when the others weren't looking.

Even I got caught up in the frenzy, and sawed a branch off our front-lawn tree, so the birds could play in a more "realistic atmosphere."

Then the second week rolled around, and things started to change. Suddenly the bird's food and water cups were empty. There was no more birdseed at the bottom of my bathtub. My oldest decided to buy a CD with her money instead. When I asked my youngest if she was excited that it was Saturday, and she could stay home with her bird, she replied, "You can play with him Mommy."

I started to guilt the children.

"You know, Tweety hasn't been out in a while. He must be lonely," I said to my middle child.

"Mom..." she said as she looked me straight in the eye, "Tweety's just a bird."

The next tactic was taken straight from the parenting book of speeches.

"You know girls," I say over dinner one night, "You guys PROMISED to take of these birds when I bought them, remember?"

Blank stares.

"Remember being in the pet store, and begging me for them? We'll feed them Mom. We'll play with them..."

Still blank.

My oldest looks over at me and says, "You know I hear

that if you set them free, they fly down to Florida, where they can survive in the wild."

* * *

So much for the birds. I now feed and water them. I change their little bird bath. I clean their cage. The other day, I crouched in our upstairs hallway with my hand in the cage trying to feed one of the birds a treat. My middle daughter came upstairs with a friend of hers.

"Mom, are you playing with Tweety?"

I stare blankly at her, trying to process the fact that she still knows "her" bird's name. I nod my head.

"You know, you really should ask me first," she says, and takes her friend into her room.

I stand in our hallway for at least 15 minutes before I can rejoin the general population of our household for fear of exploding. I have decided to never take my kids to the pet store again.

Six months later my middle daughter brings home a paper from school. They are in desperate need of someone to adopt the class rat, as one of the children is allergic to it. She starts the speech.

"I swear, Mom, I will feed him every day!"

"No!" I say determinedly.

"I will use my own allowance to buy his food!"

"No."

I will clean him and water him and...."

"No."

"But he needs a home, or he'll be an orphan. He'll be sad and lonely and...."

"No."

* * *

Every night now as I cover the birds, I check on Chester the rat...just to make sure he's been fed and watered. He is a very nice rat and feels right at home in our pet orphanage.

Myth:
My Baby Is a Genius!

Chapter three

Babies

For the same reason animals make it into your home, I think God made babies so cute so that you and your mate wouldn't think about what you were *really* getting yourselves into. My babies are eight, nine and 13 now, and not nearly as cute as before they walked and talked.

Don't get me wrong, my children are beautiful, wonderful human beings whom I love. It's just they no longer think I know what I'm talking about. When they were little, every word out of my mouth was like gold. Every idea I had was brilliant. Now I am like the resident circus clown: amusing to watch, yet commanding little respect.

The other day I got into an argument with my oldest about three-way calling. She insisted that it didn't cost us a dime, and that it was covered under our phone company's calling plan. I tried to remain calm, and just simply tell her that it wasn't true.

"Fifty cents, every time you use it," is what I tell her.

She does not buy this, so I go to grab a copy of our last phone bill. Somehow in my naivete, I think this will be enough proof.

"None of my friends pays for three-way calling," she says to me smugly.

I inform her that none of her friends sees the actual phone bill, and that even if she's had a conversation with them about their calling plan (*which I doubt you have*) they wouldn't know this anyway since they don't pay any of their own bills yet. She shakes her head at me again.

"Not true! Tracey pays for her own calls."

I stupidly think that this statement might contain a lesson for her.

"You see! Aren't you lucky you're not Tracey. You don't have to pay for phone calls in our house."

I have a triumphant smile on my face, thinking that my point has come across finally.

"Well, at least she has three-way calling," my daughter says and sighs as she leaves the room.

I sit down to have a cup of coffee, and wonder which year it was that I possibly went wrong.

I have a friend who is a first time mom, of a two-and-a-half month-old. Somehow that half is very important to her. She checks the little chart the doctor gave her, every day, to make sure her baby's progress is "developmentally accurate."

"She's not rolling over yet!" she said to me the other day, with a look of fear in her eyes. I tried to explain to her that every infant does things in her own time. This is not a viable excuse for new mothers.

"But they said she should be able to push herself up, and roll over by now!"

I go for a joke.

"Just thank God the little thing can't move yet. That's when you really start to worry."

I start to laugh, until I notice that I am laughing alone. My friend looks as if she's about to cry.

"What do you mean she can't move yet? Do you think there's something wrong with her?" she says with sudden panic in her voice. Now I really want to laugh, but suppress the urge.

"No! Of course not." I say reassuringly, "She's perfectly normal!"

This does not seem to suffice, as my friend is now eyeing me suspiciously, as if I know something, but I'm just not telling her.

Later, I decide to call her just to make sure she's okay, and her husband informs me that she took the baby to the pediatrician to be checked. I try to remember those days. When my kids went to the doctor every time they sneezed, but it seems like another lifetime. Last week my oldest informed me that she had a sore throat, and I launched into my *You better be dying if I have to make a doctor's appointment* speech.

"Does it feel like strep?" I ask. "Because you know what strep feels like, and if I have to take you for a culture, you better be sure it REALLY hurts. And I don't mean just bother me hurts, I mean *I can't swallow—my tongue is numb hurts*!"

It sounds horrible and insensitive as I say it to her, but this is experience talking. I have had one of the kids to the doctor so many times for "dizziness" that the doctor pulled me aside and asked me if she was on any "substances" I didn't know about. I told him she was only seven. I had another one at an eye specialist because she ran into the side of a pool with her eye open, and broke a blood vessel. Another one was at the doctor three times in one year because she "thought she broke her foot." I know better than to take my kids to the doctor unless it will most certainly require stitches, or a breathing tube.

I guess my friend will fall into that wisdom some day, after her third child sticks an open safety pin in his mouth "to pretend it is braces" and swallows it. (By the way, there's nothing you can do, except let it pass.) She'll eventually learn that not every emergency, really is an emergency, and she'll give up on telling her children *The Boy Who Cried Wolf* story.

My friend, whose baby is now two-months-and-three-weeks has recently ordered her daughter a baby video. One where the baby is supposed to develop into a smarter, more successful baby by watching a series of black and white floating shapes set to classical music. When she tells me this, I actually do laugh. I just can't help it.

"It really works!" she says, ignoring my skepticism. "I have a friend whose baby is six months old and can already pull herself up to a standing position, and almost take a step!"

"And all this comes from floating shapes and music," I say to her sarcastically. She tells me I'm jaded, and that she'll talk to me later.

After I hang up the phone, I think back to when my kids were small. Especially my oldest, considering I had no other experiences to help me at the time. I remember thinking about how much I was going to teach her. About how she must be a genius, because she responded to the shape cards I had made for her out of 3x5 cards and construction paper. About how I swore she was starting to recognize the square, at just three months old. About how I made my own mobile, because the one's out there just weren't suited to her developmental skills. In retrospect, I think that babies don't really need to be stimulated nearly as much as we think. The time for learning comes soon enough. In fact, at three months old, she didn't learn anything from my teaching. But looking back, I think I'm the one who learned a lot from her.

When I brought my first-born home from the hospital I was scared. I wanted to do everything right. I bought fifty onesies, two hundred diapers, and stayed up late, every night boiling bottles and sterilizing pacifiers. Then reality set in. I had not slept for five weeks in a row. I had changed, fed, washed, rocked, sang to, and burped this child, and she still cried. I changed formulas, in fear of a milk intolerance, and she still cried. I had applied six different diaper rash creams in the course of a month, even though she had no visible sign of a rash, and still she cried. I stimulated her with pastel and primary colors, and still she cried. I took her out in the car, and rocked her in the swing, and sat her on top of the dryer so she could feel the motion, and still she cried. I had her to the pediatrician at least twice a week. I tried every different bottle I could find. I changed detergents, bought a heartbeat simulator machine, and set up a cool mist humidifier in her room.

Still all she did was cry.

At this point, I had a revelation. Nothing, I mean nothing, was going to stop this baby from crying. She was now five months old, and I bought a monitor, and decided to check on her periodically at night to make sure she was still breathing. Other than that, there was nothing to do. I'd love to say she stopped crying after the first few nights, but that wouldn't be true. She continued on like this until she was over a year-and-a-half. It was the longest year and a half I have ever lived.

* * *

Now let me tell you what I learned from all this.

One: That no matter how much she cried, I still loved her.

Two: That no matter how much she screamed when I gave her

a bath, nothing could feel better than holding your warm baby wrapped in a towel.

Three: On the few occasions she actually did smile at me (and it wasn't gas) the whole world was perfect and time stood still.

Four: That going out with my friends and having a good time was nothing compared to finally having her fall asleep in my arms.

Five: That no matter what I do, I will not always be able to solve all of her problems.

Six: That she had changed my whole life, forever, and that I actually liked it.

Since the time they were babies, all three of my daughters have taught me a great many lessons, each in her own way. But those first lessons still remain true. I think God gives you children in the form of helpless little babies, for more reasons than the fact that they are cute (although it doesn't hurt).

Honestly, I don't believe I taught my daughter a single thing that first year, and she never achieved genius status thanks to my instructional efforts, though she's pretty smart. Smart enough, I have to say, to have taught me a great deal over the years.

Myth:
My Children Will Learn Manners Because I Will Teach Them

Chapter four

The Nakie Parade

I am not allowed to see my children naked anymore. I do not know where or when this rule came into play; it just did. Last week I accidentally walked in on my nine-year-old getting changed, and she screamed like I had just shot her.

"What are you doing?" she yelled as she pushed me out and shut the door. I tried to apologize through the closed door, but all I heard was an impatient sigh. I don't know how this change happened without me being informed, but it appears that without warning the rules have been altered.

I am not, under any circumstance, accidental or otherwise, to witness any nakedness.

As I walk downstairs I start to think of the irony in what just happened. To fully understand how I feel, you will need a little background.

When my oldest daughter was four-and-a-half she established a tradition which is now referred to as *The Nakie Parade*. She was a possessive child, and enjoyed my complete attention at all times. One day I was on the phone trying to establish yet another payment plan for our electric bill. My daughter apparently decided I was not paying enough attention to her. She also decided that the appropriate response to my obvious indifference was to get naked and receive the kind of attention she deserved.

She was upstairs, and I was downstairs on the sofa, when she came marching down the stairs completely and utterly naked. When I say marching, I mean marching. She had a complete *Music Man* routine worked out, and did a full turn around the living room before coming over to me. She then shook her little naked rear-end in my face, cracked up, and went running back upstairs laughing the whole way.

Needless to say, I ended up giving the woman from the electric company *all* the wrong information, and had to start over again. After I hung up the phone, I called my daughter down to have a talk. Now I didn't want her to be ashamed of nakedness, and after all it was in the privacy of our own home, in front of only her mother. But I did proceed with a short speech.

"Honey, when Mommy is on the phone she needs to

concentrate, so it's better that you leave her alone, unless you really need something."

She looks at me and says, "Okay, Mommy," and walks back upstairs. I smile at her cuteness, and think of what a funny anecdote it will make later, and soon forget all about it.

Until two weeks later when one of my friends stops by for coffee, and my daughter parades down the stairs completely naked again. It is not so cute the second time, and my friend, who has no children, is visibly embarrassed. Especially when the routine ends in the rear-end shake again. After my friend leaves, I call my daughter down, to give her the next salvo in my speech arsenal.

"Honey, Mommy is allowed to visit with friends too. And Mommy doesn't want you to get naked when they come over, okay? It isn't polite to come marching downstairs naked and shake your rear-end at people, okay?"

"Okay, Mommy." she says, and I once again feel that perhaps the problem has ended.

Until the following week when I am once again on the phone. The parade starts up, only this time she has set her march to song, and is singing "The Nakie Parade, The Nakie

Parade..." over and over again. Even worse, right behind her is her one-and-a-half-year-old sister, wearing nothing but a pacifier. She is also singing, except all she gets out is a muffled, "...a-rade" at the end of each measure.

I decide that perhaps giving them too much attention might be just what they want. So I choose to ignore it. They parade several times around the room and end with the familiar shake, and then run up the stairs howling.

Over the course of the next two years, and with the addition of their third sister (a rather willing participant), *The Nakie Parade* grows. It occurs every once and a while, out of the blue, and lasts anywhere from three to twenty minutes. It always ends with the shake, the running, and the giggling.

I am thinking about all of this as I walk downstairs. I am remembering how many baths I gave my kids over the years. How many diapers I changed. How many times I said "so big" and helped them put on their P.J.'s. And how many nakie parades I had to endure.

The irony is, that at a certain point, I had to have a talk with all three of my girls, explaining the social aspects of nakedness. How preschool would be a bad place to get naked. How the mall is another bad place to get naked, or pull down Mommy's skirt so she's naked. How when a friend comes over, it's better to get changed in the bathroom. How when Mommy's friends come over, that's not a good time to be naked either.

But now, now that they're older, after worrying about my girls' impromptu exhibitions for so long, and where they might take place, I am banned from my own bathroom while my daughter is changing her shirt.

Oh, well. Thus marks the end of another innocent era in their lives. Another part of their lives that I have been denied access. I tell you, it's not the actual *Nakie Parade* that I'll miss so much. As time goes by, it's the growing up and loss of innocence that make me yearn, always, for the younger years.

Myth:
My Home Will Be Organized

Chapter five

Disorganization and Duct Tape

I used to be an optimist. You know, *a glass-half-full* kind of person. Now I'm not quite sure what I am. I'm not *a glass-half-empty*. I'm more of a *please-don't-break-the-glass* person. I guess that translates into being a realist. It's not what's in the glass I'm thinking about, it's whether or not I'm going to be the one who cleans it up when it falls.

My mother is a neat person. According to her she has been neat and tidy all her life. She has a system. Everything in her house is organized. She boasts labeled boxes. She has folders for different papers. She has all the pieces to puzzles. She even has one of those boxes you store wrapping paper in. This is not so at my house. I had one of those wrapping paper boxes once, but my kids filled it with water and mud and housed a turtle in our back yard.

It's not that over the years I haven't tried to organize. One time I bought one of those file cabinets with the hanging folders inside. I labeled all of the folders with headings like: *Car Repairs, Bank Statements* and *Medical Information.* I meant well. The problem was that I found that I didn't have the time to actually PUT the papers in there. I decided that piles on top of the fridge, and on the kitchen table, and basically, anywhere in the house where a shelf made itself handy, was more convenient. I mean who has time to organize when you're bringing home a kid with a 104° fever from the doctor, and the child is throwing up all over your husband's easy chair.

"Hold on honey! I'll hold your hair back as soon as Mommy alphabetizes her medical information file folder!"

That's just not the way the real world works. Except for at my mother's house.

In her basement, she has labeled shelving units upon which labeled boxes sit, and in those boxes are the items that actually appear on the label. I have to kick things out of the way just to get to my washing machine. She has all the original boxes that her Christmas ornaments came in. I have a cardboard box with no lid that has the lights, garland, and all my ornaments in it, just loosely thrown in. Every year when I blow the dust off the top, I figure if an ornament is broken, that it just wasn't meant to be. Mom has a bulletin board in her kitchen with every phone number she could ever possibly need, neatly written on it, organized by category. I have ripped pieces of paper hidden under my computer's keyboard. She has an actual phone book too, and what's more, she knows precisely where it is. My phone book disappeared shortly after we got it. I think it turned into a paper maché project. She has one of those little plastic drawer units with things like safety pins, and paper clips in it. When one of my kids comes to me and asks for a safety pin, a wild frenzy ensues.

"Well, did you check under the toaster? I thought I saw one there last month! Or how about the top shelf of the medicine cabinet, next to the pile of toothpaste? I think one got stuck in there a while ago."

In the end, I tell the kids that I think I know where the stapler is, and maybe that will work.

At least our disorganization has led to one good thing: ingenuity. When I can't find something, I always seem to have a clever idea of what to use in its place. Like when your child can't find her toothbrush, and you tell her to use her finger instead, just for tonight. And then when you tell her the next night to use her finger again because, somehow, you forgot to put the toothbrush on the list for your midday shopping trip.

Oops! And then the weekend comes, and you still haven't remembered the toothbrush, and your daughter gets invited to a sleepover.

"Did you pack your toothbrush?"

"No, mom...remember I don't have one anymore."

"Alright, then don't forget to pack your finger!"

Clever stuff like that.

One thing we use consistently in our house is duct tape. If your button falls off, use duct tape. If your daughter's favorite horse loses a leg, duct tape will fix it right up. If the kitchen faucet springs a leak...duct tape.

Last month my sister took me to get a massage. She gave the massage to me as a Mother's Day gift. I had never been to a massage therapist, but she told me it would be very relaxing. It started out that way.

The problem began when the massage therapist came into my room and told me to take everything off, and get under the sheet that was lying on the table. This included my jewelry. Now the month before the massage, my watch clasp had broken and rather than buy a new watch... you got it...duct tape. I simply cut a very thin strip of duct tape and taped the clasp shut. I even wound it around the clasp a good eight or nine times, just to make sure it wouldn't come open. The silver of the tape was almost identical to the silver band of my watch, and so I marveled at my own creativity.

But now, I'm standing in the middle of a spa, completely naked except for my watch. I cannot remove the duct tape.

After several showers, and countless number of dishes washed, my duct tape has formed an impenetrable bond. I decide to just leave it on, because if I don't get under the sheet soon, my therapist will march in to find me standing there naked.

Well, my massage starts, and it is indeed everything my sister said. There is a CD playing in the background, with little birds chirping and a waterfall sound and quiet music. The lights have been dimmed and I am truly feeling relaxed.

Until the therapist starts to move down my arm, and discovers my watch.

I figure that it doesn't matter, until I feel the therapist start to fiddle with the clasp. Only it's not the clasp. It's duct tape. Super-glue-bonded duct tape. So I start to say something, until I think about what to actually say.

"Oh, don't worry about getting that off, it's duct-taped to my arm!"

Instead of embarrassing myself, I decide to try to help her get it off, somehow forgetting that I wasn't able to remove it before the massage, and apparently thinking that maybe things have changed since then. But I am lying on my stomach, and can't get to it with my other hand. So I somehow decide to flip over, so I can use both hands. Only when I do, I lose my sheet, and am now completely naked.

What's worse is that the therapist has now discovered the duct tape, and I have to go into the "I duct-taped my watch to my wrist" speech anyway, and at the same time, fumble for my sheet, which has fallen on the floor.

Months later, I am fully recovered from the embarrassment of the duct tape-massage incident and have almost stopped thinking about what the massage therapist must think of me.

The other day over coffee, I thanked my sister for the massage and made sure she understood what a generous gift I thought it was. But afterward, I told her that next Mother's Day, I would prefer a new watch instead. If not, perhaps a new roll of duct tape.

Myth:
Stereotypes Are Always Difficult to Overcome

Chapter six

The Boy and the Kitten

Allowance over the years has risen to exorbitant proportions. When I was a kid, my allowance was raised a quarter per year, at the time of my birthday. If that rule still applied, my oldest daughter would have to be a hundred and sixteen years old to get the allowance she wants. She has told me, now that she's thirteen, that she needs more money for stuff. I asked her what kind of stuff, and she had a whole long list of "needs."

"Well, you know I need make-up, and hair stuff. And I have to buy my own shampoo, because you keep buying that cheap stuff. And I go out at least twice a week and need money for that. And Thursday is pizza day at school, and you make me use my own money if I want two slices. Oh, and I want to dye my hair black, and hair dye is at least eight bucks...."

I start to say something about dyeing her hair, and at the last second I stop myself. I recall an incident last year that happened in the parking lot of a local store. The girls and I were out driving around that night looking for my oldest daughter's yearbook. We had gone out to the stores earlier that day, and my daughter announced, right before bed that night that she thinks she may have left her yearbook outside. After searching for about ten seconds, she came running back inside telling me that she remembers where it is.

"That's great, Honey, go get it."

"I can't mom..."

"Why not?"

"Because I left it on the back of the car and it's not there."

"Well where is it then?"

"I think we drove to the store with it still on there..."

Which is how we all ended up in a parking lot at ten o'clock at night trying to figure out which spot we had parked in. We searched everywhere for the yearbook, and had almost given up when we heard a strange noise. We turned around and saw a very tiny, scrawny little kitten. Now my oldest daughter and I are both allergic to cats, but we also have a condition called *Bleeding Hearts Disease*. Which translated means, we suddenly felt compelled to help this kitten. When my younger two saw a car race by, and the kitten almost ran right in front of it, they too joined the crusade. Forget the yearbook, we HAD to save the kitten.

After about forty minutes of trying to catch this kitten, and having no luck, I told the girls that we needed to go.

"Come on. We have to get home. Dad probably thinks we're dead by now."

"But, Mom, we can't leave the kitten!"

"Girls, he doesn't want to come. There's nothing else we can do. Plus the store is closed now and the parking lot is almost empty. He'll be safe now."

My youngest looks at me like I'm a monster and says, "All it takes is one car, Mommy, and he could be dead!"

"Yeah," my middle one chimes in, "How would you feel, knowing it was our fault!"

I am now a cat murderer if I leave this parking lot, and so we continue the chase.

All of a sudden, my oldest daughter spots a teenager coming toward us, a teenager dressed in black, with purple spiked hair, and a nose ring. My daughter looks scared. And frankly, I'm a little nervous too, considering it's almost eleven, and we're in a dark parking lot alone. The teenage boy sees us crouching on the ground, and starts toward us. I quietly step in front of the girls, to make sure they're safe. But the boy smiles at me, and asks if everything's okay. I tell him about the cat and he says that he'll try to help. He suffers from *Bleeding Hearts Disease* too. He proceeds to chase this kitten up and down the parking lot for almost an hour. This boy has been scratched all over by the time he finally catches the kitten, and at this point I retrieve a box from my car and we put the kitten in. He then pulls out his cell phone and tells me he's going to call the animal hospital. He has the number pre-programmed into his phone.

"I've had to rescue animals before," he announces.

He talks to the emergency tech and the vet says to bring him right over, considering the kitten is very malnourished. I ask him if he wants me to take the cat considering I started this whole mess, and he says that he'll drive her over.

"You should get these guys home anyway," he says, and smiles, looking at my youngest who is now fast asleep in the front seat of the car.

"Well, thank you very much!" I say sincerely. He says that it's no problem, and that if the kitten is okay, he might just take it home to keep.

"I got like ten other cats this same way. It's a shame people just leave 'em abandoned like this."

We watch the boy drive off, and my middle daughter says, "Wow! He was so nice!" I tell her that he was, and that we have to go. On the way home I tell the girls about how I was scared at first of him, because of the way he looked.

"But he turned out to be great! I guess you shouldn't judge somebody by their appearance. What really matters is what's in here," I said, and pointed to my heart.

Later, tucking her in bed, I look at my oldest daughter and tell her that I'll help her dye her hair if she wants. "It's kind of tricky to do on your own."

She tells me that she'd like it if I helped, and we leave it at that.

When I left her room, I thought about what kind of person she might be when she's all grown-up. And I thought about the boy and the kitten. I figure if she dyes her hair orange with green stripes it doesn't matter. As long as she's got a good heart. A heart that would allow her to help a scared bunch of total strangers catch an abandoned kitten.

Myth:
If You're Perfect Enough, You Can Parent with No Regrets

Chapter seven

Guilt and The Lion King

From the moment your second child is born, you feel guilty. In my case, my second came along when my first was only three. But I soon found out that three years is plenty of time for a child to "mark his or her territory." I was marked. I was her mother, no one else's, and this new baby posed a serious threat to the established boundaries. Here of course, is where the guilt factor comes in to play.

You initially need to take care of the new baby. She is little. She cries a lot. She needs to be fed every two hours. She likes to be rocked. She needs a diaper change every hour or so, which half of the time results in a necessary bath. Bottom line is: she needs a lot of attention. This is very upsetting to your older child. Especially since parents in general "over-attention" the first-born to begin with. We have set up the first child as the Center of the Universe, and it's not a title they are eager to relinquish. This is where the trouble, and the guilt begins.

My oldest daughter's jealousy ignited the second I was taken to the hospital to give birth. She was angry that I had to leave her for this new baby everyone kept talking about.

"Mommy, why do I have to stay with Grandma? Why can't I come with you?"

"Well, Honey, Mommy is going to be very busy having a new baby, and I won't be able to take care of you."

"I'll be quiet, Mommy. You won't have to watch me at all."

"Now, that doesn't sound like much fun. You don't want to sit quiet for three whole days in a boring hospital do you? Wouldn't you be happier playing and having fun at Grandma's?"

She looked up at me through teary eyes and exclaimed, "No! I want to be with you."

So by the time we brought the baby home from the hospital, my daughter had already formed the opinion that the new baby was to be viewed as an intruder. In her mind, the baby had one purpose—to steal her mother away. She wasn't going to let that happen. So in an effort to make sure I wasn't going to forget her, my oldest started on an attention-seeking mission. She wasn't about to let me forget her for a second.

I was giving the baby a bath one day, and my oldest walked in and asked me to make paper airplanes with her.

"I can't yet, Honey; Mommy's busy. How about when your sister takes her nap?"

"Fine." she said, and walked away sulking.

Two minutes later, she walked back in. "Can you read me a book?"

"A little bit later, Sweetie."

"How about we play the horsy game?"

"Not now."

"Do you want to watch a movie?"

"I can't yet."

"Marbles?"

"No."

"Dinosaurs?"

"No."

"Do you want to paint a picture?"

I looked at her and raised my voice a little.

"Honey, I told you. I can't right now. You are going to have to wait until later."

"Fine." Again she walked away sulking.

As she walked away I felt incredibly guilty, and even a little sad too. After all, for three years all my time and attention had been solely devoted to this child, and now I was trying to toggle between two little ones and be the best I could be, for both children.

So when my oldest came to me later that day and asked

if we could pretend we were lions, I said that I would love to. The baby was down for her nap, and I had a chance to play. I was very happy to finally have this time together, and so I got down on all fours and started to roar. My daughter laughed and joined in, until we were both roaring at the top of our lungs and chasing each other around the living room. We both forgot all about the new baby sleeping, if only for a brief moment.

This is the moment my husband walked in from work. My daughter is now up on the back of the sofa, attempting a reenactment of the final scene in Disney's *The Lion King*, where all the lions roar back and forth to each other. I am at the foot of the sofa, representing the rest of the pride. We are roaring to one another so loudly that we don't even hear the door open.

"What are you two doing?" he says.

We both stop roaring, and start giggling. My husband looks at me like we're nuts, and then puts his finger to his lips and says, "Shhh!"

Deep silence. But only for a split second. We all hear the baby, crying loudly upstairs. I suddenly feel like a child who's been caught doing something they shouldn't, as my husband goes to get the baby from her crib. My oldest looks over at me sadly and says, "I guess were done now." She gets up and walks away, and I am now dealing with a double-dose of guilt.

When my husband brings the baby down, her face is beet red like she's been crying for a while. In the meantime, my oldest has gone to her room to "play alone." And I am sitting on the sofa thinking about how both of the kids are upset now, and trying to figure out how to juggle a family.

Over the course of the next few months, I try everything in my power to successfully split my time, so both my kids get enough attention. I feed the baby with one hand while trying to do origami with the other. I give the baby a bath, while trying to splash my oldest playfully so she doesn't feel left out. I buy one of those front pack baby carriers, so I can dance around with my oldest, with the baby carefully strapped to me. I manage to glue the legs on a paper spider, while changing a diaper at the same time. I can even cook dinner, talk on the phone, while singing to the baby in her infant seat, AND pretend I'm a Tyrannosaurus Rex stomping on a Lego town, all at the same time.

I am Super Mom! I am invincible!

The only problem is that I have developed dark circles under my eyes, and a slight twitch in my shoulder. I have two different shoes on at all times, and I haven't showered in over a week. My husband keeps looking at my hair, which has been in the same ponytail for days, and he asks me when was the last time I changed my clothes.

"No time." I say. "Gotta go pretend I'm the witch, and steal the golden candles from the princess's castle."

He looks at me funny, and asks me if I want to come sit down for a little bit and watch TV. I look at my watch and then at him like he's crazy.

"*Barney* is on in 22 minutes, and I promised I'd watch it.

But before that I have to read a book and do the witch thing while I wash the baby's hair. I will have to see you later."

That night in bed, my husband finally breaks down and tells me that I need a shower.

"Honey, I'm not trying to be mean, but you have been wearing a moo-moo for over a week now, and I'm afraid that your hair won't even come out of that ponytail if you don't wash it soon. You really need to slow down and take care of yourself a little."

In my disabled state of mind, this was the wrong thing to say. So I spend the next hour loudly explaining to him the newfound challenges of children and time management.

"Slow down! Slow down! HA! How in the world do you expect me to slow down?!! I barely have the time to cook dinner, much less take a shower! Do you realize that I have had clean clothes sitting on the bathroom counter for a week now! Every time I even take a step towards the shower something happens! The baby wakes up, or the video ends, or the phone rings, or it's time for a meal! I can't even do it before bed, cause by that time the baby is awake again and needs to be fed! Or the other one wakes up scared, and I have to lie with her until she goes back to sleep! And by that time the baby has pooped one of those poops that require changing her diaper, clothes, and all the bed sheets!! Do you understand??? There is no RIGHT TIME anymore!!!"

My husband, who is a wonderful man, tells me that it's going to be okay.

"I just need to pitch in more, that's all. When I get home from work, I'll watch the kids so you can go shower, okay? You're a great mom. You just have to try to stop being a Super Mom. No one can do that for too long, Honey. You need to slow down, for your own sanity...."

I burst into tears when he finishes, and tell him all about the guilt.

"Every time I try to leave them for even a second, they need something. And when I spend too much time feeding the baby, the other one gets jealous. So I have to spend time with her too. It's a vicious cycle. And I never get a shower...."

I am bawling in his arms, and when I finally settle down, I tell him that I'm going to jump in the shower now. He smiles and kisses me, and tells me that sounds like a good idea.

Since that night, a long time ago, things have changed significantly. By the time my third daughter was born, I had slowed down a great deal. My oldest one was in kindergarten by then, and my second one was only sixteen months old. I had no time to worry about who got played with enough—I was just happy when we had clean clothes in the house. If they all got dressed and fed, in the course of a day, I considered it a triumph. I think this is why my youngest seems so well adjusted. She never got the chance to have me all to herself. The thought never even crossed her mind.

Even my oldest finally came to terms with the invasion of her younger sisters, and accepted that I could be mom to all three of them. I still get pangs of guilt here and there. When one of them tries to talk when the other one is talking first and I have to tell them to wait their turn. They all get that sulking look on their faces. The same one my oldest used to get when the baby woke up and took me away from her.

But all in all we are a family now, and we share our time and energies together.

One of my favorite things is to simply watch them play together. When they wrestle around on the living room floor. Or when they stick up for each other in front of their friends. Or just simply when they laugh together. They are sisters, and all the mommies in the world can't alter that. I know there are times when each child would like me all to herself. And there are plenty of times I would like to spend one-on-one time with each of them. But I have come to a general understanding that I can't be every thing, to every one, at every time.

I also came to an understanding years ago, that normal people do indeed wash, on a regular basis, and that I could too, if I tried hard enough. So now at least I can shower without guilt. And as for sharing Mommy equally among my offspring and spouse...I do the best job I can, one imperfect day at a time.

Myth:
I Will Always Meet Their Basic Needs: Food, Shelter, and Clean Clothes…

Chapter eight

The Laundry Mystery

We wash very few actual clothes in our house. We try, mind you. We fill the washer until it's reached its capacity and then let it do its job. We then place that so-called entire load in the dryer, and let it spin until dry. The results, however, are not clean clothes that the children can wear. I would say only one-quarter of what comes out of this process actually belongs to our kids. And half of the 25% turns out to be clothes they've outgrown or dislike, most of the time still folded from a previous washing.

The rest of what is clean is divided along these lines...

Approximately 25% is other children's clothes. Kids

who have slept over, kids who just came to visit, kids who wandered in to use the phone, perhaps even children who drop off their laundry for a free cleaning. Who knows who these children actually are, because when I individually ask my kids to identify the mystery clothing, I always get the same answer: "I don't know. Why are you asking me?" I always want to respond to that by telling them that Dad and I don't bring home guests that are a children's size 8/10, but I bite my tongue. This pile of clean clothes generally sits on my stairs, for months at a time. It is our own personal Lost and Found, and we are still working on the found part of that.

That means every small visitor to our home gets interrogated.

"Honey, can you come look at these clothes and see if any are yours?"

Glance at the clothes mound.

"Nope."

"Are you sure, Sweetie? Take another quick peek."

"Nope."

"They're clean. Maybe you just don't recognize them cleaned up like this?"

"Nope."

"Well, would you like to take some home anyway? It's a shame to let them go to waste."

"Nope."

I have a small consignment shop's worth of mystery clothes to date, and thus far no takers.

The next 25% of the laundry is clothes, but they don't belong to human beings. This portion belongs to plush toys and dolls. We frequently make sure that Barbie has clean clothes to surprise Ken. Or that our kids' baby dolls have a clean bib and blanket. Of course the stuffed animals get in on the deal, too. Sometimes just their clothes, sometimes the animal itself.

Apparently when we ask our children to gather up their laundry, something is lost in the translation. In their language it means gather up the laundry, along with anything that might be Velcroed to the laundry, under the laundry, mixed in with the laundry, or too annoying to remove from the laundry. On a positive note, though, none of our stuffed animals ever smells funny, even if they are all slightly misshapen. And Barbie never looked so good.

The next 15%-25% of our laundry consists of pocket contents. A pen or crayon. An old lollipop. A tissue. A lip-gloss that magically opens in the dryer. A missing credit card. Dad's bank statement. Basically anything that is in our house, purse, wallet or car, is fair game. The rules surrounding these items are still somewhat unclear, but one thing for sure is, they will either be an important artifact, or make a tremendous mess, whichever is more inconvenient at the time. On a side note, a little practical advice you might consider is to encourage your children to concentrate on carrying non-dangerous items in their pockets.

Crayons, lipstick, glue, pens, hamsters, bubblegum,

stickers, wax, printer ribbons, frogs, powdered Kool-Aid, food coloring and marshmallow bunnies, all make the list as problem items.

If I could go back and do it over, I would explain this list to my children in detail from the time they were very young. It may be too late for me, but not for some of you. I suggest if your kids have already passed the age of listening, that you either stuff their pockets so full of paper products that nothing else will fit, sew all pockets shut, or allot an enormous budget for clothing purchases each year (oh, and start a new dryer fund while you're at it).

Of course this breakdown of laundry contents is subject to slight variations. Sometimes what's washed consists of mainly toys. Sometimes 10% or more might be electronics, or tax return paperwork. Sometimes a small but significant sheaf of homework papers or tests are in the mix, always documents that were supposed to be signed. The breakdown varies, but one thing remains the same. After washing ten loads or so, the children will still complain that there's nothing to wear.

When you try to explain to them the surprising ratio of their clothes to other items, they will just stare at you blankly. Better to save your breath for other battles. Perhaps even battles you might win.

I know that some of you are thinking that we're not doing a very good job of checking the laundry more carefully before we wash it. Maybe that's true. I had a dream once that we could achieve that. But just like so many other dreams regarding organization lists for our house, that fantasy died a long time ago. If I can find a moment in between everything else in life, to actually put a load of laundry in, I'll be darned if I'm going to waste more time checking it.

I'm not knocking you, by the way, if you have a system in your home that works. If you have pants without juice stains on them, or shirts without eye-liner melted into them, more power to you. If you've never washed a family pet, or melted super-glue in your dryer, good for you. For me, however, I'm just happy if my kids go to school not naked, whether I have to give them something from the mystery stairs pile to wear, or try to squeeze them into a Barbie outfit.

Post script: If you are ever in rural Pennsylvania, and believe any of your children could have possibly visited our home, please stop by and refer to the list of Lost-and-Found items posted on my front door. Even if it's an impossibility that the item is your child's, check the size list anyway. We have a great many 8/10's and 10/12's that could use a good home. If you are looking for clothes with no stains, however, you need not inquire.

Otherwise, please help! My stairs are practically impassable. Thank you.

Myth:
My Children Will Never Question My Love for Them

Chapter nine

Delivered by the Mailman?

One day after school my youngest walks in looking as if she is about to cry. Being six at the time, and still loving school, she immediately made me concerned.

"What's wrong? Did you have a fight with a friend?" I ask sincerely.

"No."

"Did you get in trouble today?"

"No!"

"Then what, Honey?"

My daughter bursts into tears.

"I'm not adopted!"

I am completely stunned. In all the magazines on child-rearing I've read over the years, all the empathetic chats with other parents, every theme Oprah has covered, I have never encountered the "Children Who Are Upset Because Their Parents Didn't Adopt Them" topic. This problem then being unfamiliar territory, I decided I would need much more information before offering up any condolences.

"Honey, I'm not sure what you're trying to say here."

"You didn't pick me!"

"Well of course we didn't pick you, Honey, because God gave you to us."

"See, you didn't have a choice!"

Since my daughter is only six, I decide not to go into the specifics of what role humans play in God's decision, and decide only to calm her instead.

"Sweetie, we wanted you, that's what's important! Where is all this adoption stuff coming from anyway?"

My daughter proceeds to tell me about her Show-and-Tell that day at school. One of the children in her class had brought in a photograph of his parents. At first, all the children had been skeptical as to why a picture of Mom and Dad would qualify as an interesting Show-and-Tell, and one of the kids even let out a snoring noise when the boy had gotten up to speak. But when the boy started his story, the children changed their tune. The room fell into a hush and all ears were riveted on the speaker.

The boy had been born in Chilé and his mother had

passed away shortly after he was born. His father was killed in an automobile accident when he was just two months old and so the boy had gone to live at a local orphanage. His adoptive parents had relatives in Chilé and had come to the orphanage when they were in the country visiting family. They immediately picked the boy out of a roomful of children, and started the adoption proceedings the very same day. The boy in front of the class finished his Show-and-Tell by saying that his parents loved him so much, because even though they could've singled out any child in the room that day, they had picked him.

A beautiful story of triumph and love, I thought to myself. But I still wasn't quite sure how this story factored into our lives, and why it was so distressing to my daughter.

"Honey, that's a wonderful story. I'm so glad your friend found a family who loves him, but I'm still not exactly sure why the story upset you so much?"

"Because I'm not adopted."

"And...?"

"How do I know how much you love me?"

Now I understood what my daughter meant. She wasn't upset that she wasn't adopted; she was upset that she didn't have a tangible reason demonstrating our love for her. After all, the little boy had been chosen out of dozens of children, and to this little boy, that was a wonderful expression of love that he would always have to hold on to.

"Oh, Honey, I think I understand now. You think that if

we didn't pick you out, maybe we didn't really want you?"

Tears welled up in my daughter's eyes, as she shook her head up and down.

"Of course we wanted you!"

"But how do I know that?"

"Well, we kept you didn't we? That's got to count for something."

"Yeah, except Mrs. Tulley and you were talking one day, and you told her that I was a surprise."

Over the years, with all the ignoring children do when you are speaking directly to them, you forget how much listening they do when you're not.

"Oh, but surprises can be wonderful, can't they? What about surprises on your birthday? You like those, don't you?" "Yeah…" she paused. But it wasn't your birthday."

I decided to take a different approach. One that would positively fall into the parameters of what a six-year-old could comprehend.

"Okay. So you want to know how much I love you, is that right?"

My daughter's eyes curiously searched my face as she said yes.

"Alright, what's my favorite food in the world?"

"Lobster!"

"Right! And what's my favorite hobby?"

"I think it's...writing?"

"Exactly! How about my favorite thing to do at the

beach?"

"Kite-flying?"

"Uh-huh. And how about my favorite children's book? *"You Are Special!"*

"Yup!"

I went on to ask her about my favorite movie, my favorite animal, my favorite color, my favorite singer, and every other favorite thing I could think of.

"Yeah, but Mommy, what does all this have to do with me? Are you just doing that thing where you make me think about something else, so I forget what I was sad about?"

"No, Honey, just listen. Let's pretend the mailman came one day and put an enormous box on the front porch. What would I think?"

"You'd get mad at Daddy for ordering something?"

"No, Sweetie. Focus. Pretend I opened that box and inside was a big plate of lobster, a brand new kite, all the albums Josh Groban ever made, a bouquet of hyacinths, a brand new puppy, and everything else Mommy likes."

"Like all your favorite things?"

"Yes, all my favorite things, just sitting there, in one box."

"WOW! That'd be cool."

"Yes it would. But listen, pretend there was another box sitting next to the first, and I decided to open that one too, and when I opened the cover, you popped out!"

"That would be funny! You'd get scared!"

"Yes, I probably would...but pretend the mailman told me that I had to return one of those two boxes; that I was only allowed to keep one, and the other one had to go back. Okay?"

My daughter's eyes widened at the thought.

"I want you to know, Honey, that I wouldn't even have to think about it. That I would tell the mailman to take back the box with my favorite things in it, because I would rather keep you."

"You would?"

"Of course I would! Nothing is more important than you! Not even all the lobster in the world!"

My daughter threw her arms around me and told me that she loved me, and that she would never return me to the mailman either. In her simple, childish way, she understood that even though I hadn't selected her from an orphanage, I wouldn't trade her for anything.

That night I walked in on my daughter emptying a box that had been sitting in her closet.

"What are you doing, Sweetie?"

"Oh, I want to take this box to school tomorrow for Show-and-Tell. I want to tell all the kids about how the mailman dropped me off on the porch one day, and how you kept me, even though you could've had, what's-his-name, Groban!"

I smiled, and after straightening the story out for her slightly, I sent her off to bed. She did take that box in for Show-and-Tell the next day and, later in the week, I received an email from my daughter's teacher.

"I enjoyed your daughter's presentation on Tuesday; it is apparent that she feels quite loved at home. However, I think she may be slightly confused as to how she came to be a part of your family, and might need to have things clarified for her again."

I did speak to my daughter again, and eventually we got the subject all straightened out, but I saved that email from her teacher. I like to look it over occasionally; especially the part that said she feels quite loved at home.

Whether she was chosen from an orphanage or mailed to us on the front porch; whether planned or a complete surprise, my youngest daughter was one special delivery. And all I need to know is that she understands how much she really is loved.

Myth:
Mother's Day Is All About You

Chapter ten

Beautiful Dreams and Bubble Baths

New mother, do not fool yourself into believing that this day set aside for moms, this nationally recognized holiday in America, is a day of rest. Also, keep your expectations low, that way you don't have too far to fall, if you should be disappointed.

I know a few mothers who believe that this day, above all, should be a day of relaxation. That the day should start with sleeping in late, followed by breakfast in bed. Then you should get up to a perfectly clean house and be taken out to lunch at the restaurant of your choice, where your adoring family will bestow gifts upon you...sentimental cards and handwritten poems praising the wonders of you from your children. A gold necklace with your children's birthstone pendants from your adoring husband.

After lunch, you should go home and relax the afternoon away in a dreamy bubble bath, while your husband plays for hours with the kids on the lawn. Dinner will not only be made, but all the dishes will be done, and the kitchen left sparkling. Your family will have baked you a cake with World's Greatest Mom written on top, and you will never have to move from the sofa when it's the children's bedtime. They will simply kiss you and say goodnight, and they will not fight in the bathroom upstairs as they brush their teeth.

After all, it's Mother's Day.

I used to dream up phrases that my family would use on this most sacred of days. Things like: "Don't get up, Mommy, I'll get that for you." Or "Not today, Dear Mother, it's your day off." Oh, the dreams I used to have of what the day would be...

WARNING—BEWARE OF READING FURTHER if you have no children, and you plan to, and your view of Mother's Day is very closely related to the view I've just presented, do not, I repeat, DO NOT read on. Save your beautiful dreams and skip to the next chapter.

* * *

I assume if you are still reading this, you have a family, maybe a couple of children, and have already realized that only television shows from the 1950s and 60s can do justice to Mother's Day. Real life in today's world is a whole lot different. To illustrate my point, I will tell you the story of Mother's Day at my house, the year before last.

The day started like this...

I was sleeping peacefully and soundly in my bed that morning. It was beautiful. My dreams were cut short however when my youngest daughter blew a party horn in my face and screamed "Happy Mother's Day!" at the top of her lungs. I jumped a mile out of my bed, and noticed that my clock read 5:48 in the morning. I then was passed a plate full of ring bologna covered in cheddar cheese sprayed from a can.

"Look, Mommy! Breakfast in bed!"

I didn't have the heart to tell her that not since high school had I eaten anything so awful for breakfast, so with one eye open I choked the bologna down and tried to smile.

"Delicious, Honey. Thank you, really," I said, and tried to go back to sleep.

"What about your dessert?"

"Honey, we don't have dessert after breakfast."

"I know. But today's a special day, so you get dessert!"

She handed me a small bowl with two cookies, three jellybeans, a handful of peanuts, and half of a chocolate bar.

"Where's the other half?" I asked with my mouth half full.

"Oh, I had dessert too—because it's a special day!"

After finishing eating, I decided to get out of bed for

two reasons. First, I needed to take some antacid tablets after my breakfast and dessert, and second, I didn't want that horn-blower giving me a heart attack again. My daughter was thrilled that I wanted to start my special day already. My husband remained asleep through all the fun, apparently able to go deaf at will.

When we got downstairs, my other kids were already watching cartoons. My middle daughter handed me the strongest cup of coffee I have had in my whole life. A full mug that probably resembled a triple espresso you might find in a Turkish bazaar.

"Here, Mom. I made this for you!"

I thanked her and sat down, and tried to smile while I washed down four antacid tablets with the thick, murky coffee. She kept asking me if the coffee was good, and I kept smiling and thanking her. My oldest turned to me.

"Are we gonna have breakfast soon? I'm starving! Are you making pancakes? I could really go for pancakes."

I wanted to say, "Hey, wait a minute...this is supposed to be my day." But I figured I was already awake, and my indigestion felt a little better when I stood up, so why not? I made the girls pancakes and served it to them in the living room. My husband finally got up, and we all started to get ready for church. I took another antacid before we piled in the car, and I smiled at how pretty all three kids looked in their Sunday best. Even if they had grumbled when I asked them to dress nicely.

All the way to church, they fought in the car over who

did the nicer thing for me this morning.

"Yeah, well, I made her coffee. She loves coffee."

"But I took her breakfast in bed, with dessert."

"I left her alone. That definitely counts for something."

I finally chimed in.

"Girls, I thank all of you, but you know what would make me really happy? I would love it if you girls would not fight today, okay? And just be kind to each other."

The car was quiet for a minute, while each of them pondered the enormity of that request.

"Okay, Mommy. We won't fight," my youngest offered. The other girls agreed too, and we made it to church almost without incident.

After the service, the kids complained again that they were hungry and we set out to find a restaurant. We couldn't go to my favorite restaurant, because the girls don't like seafood, so I settled for a small Italian eatery (i.e.: a place where they serve pizza). First, the children had to fight over who got to sit next to me, a scuffle my husband skillfully refereed, then we finally ordered.

The kids took pizza (what a surprise), while I ordered chicken parmesan and spaghetti. After two spilled drinks, and an argument over the crayons on the table, our meals finally arrived.

"Mom, can I try your chicken?" my middle daughter asked.

"Hey, can I try it too?" my youngest chimed in.

I reluctantly handed them each a portion, trying hard to bite my tongue, and not ask why the children didn't order chicken, too, if they wanted it so badly. After the kids devoured most of my chicken and asked for some spaghetti, I just gave up and ate a slice of pizza. My stomach was still processing "breakfast" anyway.

During the car ride home, my littlest made a point of tattling on her sisters.

"They're fighting, Mom, and you said no fighting today."

I started to explain to her that I didn't want to hear about more Mother's Day bickering, but decided mid-sentence to forget the Mother's Day angle, since that seemed to be the source of their constant feuding.

"Just try to get along, please. Remember how you all promised to not fight?"

"Well I was trying, but they're not, so don't get mad at me."

The rest of the afternoon was filled with assorted mishaps and squabbles. I didn't get to take a bubble bath. I spent my time playing charades and a long game of Monopoly, which ended when my oldest accused her sisters of cheating. I finally had reached my point of breaking after trying to drink a second cup of Turkish sludge water, and asked my husband quietly to take the kids out to the park.

"But I don't want to go to the park! I want to stay with Mommy! It's Mother's Day!"

My husband intervened. "Mommy's going to relax for a while girls, so let's go, okay?"

They begrudgingly got their shoes on, and trudged toward the front door. My youngest waved goodbye sadly as she left. I sat down on the sofa and tried to soak in all the peace and quiet. But the look my daughter gave me walking out the door, made me all of a sudden feel sad. They didn't know what to do on Mother's Day. They didn't know exactly how to show their love. All they knew is that they wanted to be with me.

Over the next hour, I did enjoy relaxing, but I also found myself watching the clock for when the girls would be back.

I got big hugs and kisses that Mother's Day night. I also got several cards, two poems, a painted pot with a plant in it, a clay bowl made in art class, and a #1 Mom placemat. All handmade. All from my girls.

After I washed a few dishes, and went up to quiet the girls down in bed a second time, I came down and looked through my presents again. And I cried as I read the wonderful things my daughters had written. My oldest had written me a note telling me how thankful she was to have me as her mom. My middle daughter wrote me a poem, and the last line was, "I am lucky to have a mom who listens to me." And my youngest wrote a card that said, "Do you know how much I love you?" on the front. On the inside it said, "I love you more than all the M&M's in the world, and more than all the horses (every kind)!"

Now, how can you beat presents like that?

This year when Mother's Day rolled around, I had no expectations, no preconceived ideas of how it should go. My kids still fought. I still got breakfast in bed (although this year it was peanut butter crackers and purple Kool-Aid). Dessert was gummy worms on a dessert shell. They still argued over wearing dresses. I still took antacid more than once. I had to play baseball instead of Monopoly. I never did get the bubble bath dreams are made of. But at the end of the day, I had some of the most wonderful treasures in the world, handmade cards and notes from all my girls. That truly made it a wonderful Mother's Day.

I joke sometimes about how, in the 21st century, Mother's Day would make more sense if we renamed it Kids' Day. But really, when you think about it, from their moment of birth (and long before), kids are what being a mother is all about. Aren't they?

Myth:
I Will Help My Children Outgrow Their Fears

Chapter eleven

Venus Flytraps and Party Balloons

When your children are young, they experience many moments of irrational fear. Personally, I have given hundreds of midnight speeches where the moral of my story ends with "There's nothing to be afraid of because monsters are not real."

The speech varies of course. Instead of monsters, it could be the Boogieman, witches, carnivorous dinosaurs, enormous, flesh-eating spiders, Dracula, mummies, zombies, Godzilla, King Kong, or any number of other universally scary characters with the potential to nurture childhood nightmares.

One night, my middle daughter woke with a nightmare. I came into her room, settled her down, and asked her the ever-risky question.

"What are you afraid of, Honey?"

This particular night, it was Venus Flytraps. She had caught the very end of *Little Shop of Horrors* on cable TV that afternoon, and had simultaneously been studying plant life in school, and of course, put the two together. She concluded that Venus Flytraps were going to sneak into her room at night and swallow her whole. She also had experienced an extra dose of panic when she had to visit the bathroom and become fearful that an ivy plant we had on the counter was going to strangle her.

By the time I reached her, she was so afraid of all plant life in general that I had to promise I would immediately remove all greenery in our home.

After a good deal of tears and finally just lying down with her until she drifted off, I was able to go back to bed. Of course that was only after removing every ficus tree, peace plant, palm, fern and lily from our home and relocating them on our front porch.

The next morning, in the light of day, my daughter laughed over her dream, and stated clearly that she was no longer afraid of plants. After she left for school I skeptically brought in our miscellaneous houseplants, and hoped that the nightmare had been laid to rest.

That night as I was just drifting off comfortably settled in my bed, the door to my room was flung open to reveal my middle daughter in hysterical tears. She could barely form a sentence.

"You...you...put back...the ivy!"

Now, any parent knows there are times when, even though your child is incredibly upset, what they say is so amusing it is almost impossible not to laugh. As insensitive as it may seem, this was one of those times. So, without even being aware of it, I went to hug her and accidentally let out a chuckle. My daughter looked at me incredulously and said what most kids say.

"It's not funny!"

Again, having very little self-control at one o'clock in the morning, I stifle a giggle.

She, in turn, becomes more adamant.

"It's not funny!!!"

"I know!" I say, now on the brink of full-blown laughter, mentally picturing our 4-inch ivy plant dragging her out the window. "I'm sorry, Honey...."

The look she gives me is so serious, that I break into short bursts of silent laughter while I try to cover my mouth so she won't see. She of course notices tears coming down my cheeks, and that I haven't taken a breath for a full thirty seconds.

"You're still laughing! I told you it's not funny! You're being mean!"

Well there's nothing that sobers you up quicker than being told that you're a mean mommy. So I settle down and get myself under control, and hug her.

"I'm really sorry for laughing, Honey. It's just that you startled me with the door and I was still half-asleep and...."

Well, she forgave me for my insensitivity at that point, and after the familiar speech about "nothing to be afraid of" and promises to stay with her, she settled down and fell asleep.

The plant dreams continued over the course of a few weeks until, like most irrational childhood fears, they simply went away. There was no big announcement about their departure, no important realization my daughter came to, the dreams just ceased.

A few months later at the typical witching hour, I was awakened by what sounded like crying. I went to my middle daughter's room and found her tearful and frightened sitting up in her bed.

"What's the matter?"

"I'm scared."

"What are you scared of?"

Well this time it was The Sandman. A friend at school had told her that The Sandman comes in your room at night and sprinkles you with sand until you fall asleep. Sounds harmless enough, except my daughter had gone through a bad incident that summer at the beach when she had received a face full of sand that had gotten in her eyes. So now she was frightened of not only sand in general, but of some strange man sneaking into her bedroom at night—a man carrying buckets of sand to throw in her face.

It didn't help that we have a sandbox in our backyard,

right below her bedroom window, a fixture she strongly felt was the possible origin of The Sandman. So I started in on the familiar speech.

"Sweetie, The Sandman is not real. He can't hurt you because he's not real. He's like a character you might read about in a fairy tale. He was just made up in someone's imagination, and imaginary things can never hurt you."

While I spoke, I helped my daughter back under the covers, and told her that I would sit with her until she felt better. I moved over to the side of her bed, and while doing so stepped on something lightweight and squishy. Instantly I heard a loud "POP!" and was so startled I let out a yell and threw the stuffed animal I was holding straight up into the air. I looked down to discover that I had stepped on a balloon my daughter had brought home from a birthday party the week before.

Now, I am not a fan of balloons in general, so after shrieking, I put my hand over my mouth and let out a relieved breath. This is the exact moment that I glance over at my daughter, and notice her hand is over her mouth and her eyes have a half-glazed expression. Thinking she is frightened again, I start over the ongoing process of settling her down.

“It’s okay, Honey. It was just a balloon.”

She makes no reply, and now I start to worry that I am going to have to grab my pillow and make it a sleepover. But there is something strange about her expression, which leads me to wonder.

"Honey? Honey, can you answer me? Are you okay?"

This is the instant when I detect a slight vibration rumbling through her mattress, and at closer observation I notice the corners of her eyes are turned up.

She is not afraid. She is laughing at me.

"Are you laughing?"

There is no answer; however, the shaking of the bed becomes more intense.

"You are! You're laughing at me!"

At this point there is a series of stifled snorts mingled with short bursts of laughter.

"Oh, so it's funny when Mommy gets scared?"

"Well…it was just a…balloon!"

"Oh I see, plants and monsters are scary, but balloons are just plain funny."

I decide to go into a thorough explanation of why the balloon scared me, but this just induces a full-fledged riot of laughter. I smile at her as I get up from her bed.

"Well, it's obvious you're okay now. I'll leave you to get to sleep, Silly!"

As I get up, my daughter quickly sobers up.

"Don't leave Mommy! I'm still scared!"

"But, Honey, you're okay now. You were laughing. See, we learned a good lesson out of all this, that something can scare us only if we let it. But if we laugh about it, then the fears can go away."

While my speech sounds reasonable in words, practical

application is much harder, and after seeing her intense, pleading expression, I climb back into bed and tell her I will stay with her.

We lie silently for a little while, until my daughter leans over and whispers in my ear.

"What else are you scared of, Mommy, besides balloons?"

I want to say that the balloon had just startled me, not actually scared me. I want to tell her that her big brave Mom wasn't really scared of anything. In reality, though, that isn't true. I am afraid sometimes. Some fears are rational; others are just plain silly. Still, at my age, it's sometimes hard to separate the two.

"I'm afraid of thunder sometimes," I say quietly.

"No way! So am I! What else?"

"Spiders."

"Me too! I'm afraid of wasps, bees and yellow jackets too."

"I don't like them either."

My daughter moves over and cuddles up to me.

"I'm so glad I'm not the only one afraid, Mom."

That night, my daughter finally drifted off to sleep, and I lay there thinking about fear. I have no magic potion that will ever cure her of all her ghostly fantasies, or foolish nighttime trepidations. I certainly possess no potion that will cure her for life.

Whether a human being is nine or 90, I'd be willing to

bet they have something they are afraid of. Lying there, the only thing I knew for sure was that for that night, for that one night, I was her magic potion. The one thing that made it okay for her to fall asleep was knowing that I was there to keep her safe, and the thing that helped her to feel better was knowing that I too had fears. That I was as vulnerable as she.

I would venture to say that throughout my daughter's life she'll grow in and out of fears, regardless of my attempts to calm them. Whether she's nine or 90, what she may need most is someone willing to stay with her when she's afraid, and remind her that she is not alone. I wish her that comfort, fervently, at some moment in the distant future when fear closes in and I can't be there.

Myth:
I Will Maintain My Sense of Self

Chapter twelve

Identity Crisis

Any mother knows that as soon as you have children, you lose a good deal of your identity. You are no longer a teacher or a nurse or a lawyer or a technician. You no longer have hobbies like sailing, or bicycling or hiking or sewing. You are a parent. That's what you do: you parent. Day in and day out, you parent.

If it's a Saturday night, and you've had tickets to a Broadway play for three months, and a babysitter is in your living room and you are dressed in a beautiful new dress, and your eight-year-old throws up...you stay home and parent. If your favorite football player of all time is going to be at your local bank signing his new book, and your daughter has a soccer game at the same time, you parent. If you have to arrange to trade your co-worker every one of his Saturday shifts for a month, so you can go to your kid's class play at school, that's what you do. You parent.

Likewise, when your children begin to get older, every parent discovers, after all the years of having virtually no identity, you quietly develop the urge to get one back. At first you just want a little identity. You might want to, once a month, go out alone with a friend. Or every other week, take a night pottery class. Or get back into karate, or photography or jogging. Or go on a cruise—one where you don't stuff half of your luggage with toys for the trip. Or how about grocery shopping alone for a change of pace?

I have a bit of advice to parents who have reached the point of revisiting your identity.

Beware. Though they have ignored you for weeks, your offspring will display mysterious signs of interest in your newfound search for identity and independence.

Suddenly, children who have spent months telling you you're not needed, that you're always wrong about something, resent you for leaving them. Suddenly, the child who spends most of her time on the phone ignoring you is concerned about where you're going. Suddenly, your littlest wants to sit on your lap every time you sit down to sew, or read or write.

I told my oldest daughter last week that I would love to take a ballroom dancing class. To this she replied, "I like ballroom dancing."

I looked at her and said, "Not once have you ever even mentioned liking ballroom dancing."

"Well, I do. I could come with you, you know, and be your partner," she said, smiling a hopeful smile. I told her I'd think about it.

That night I told my husband about the ballroom dancing class.

"Well, Honey, if you really want to do it, go for it."

"I just might. The only thing is that when I mentioned it, our oldest suddenly and without warning also developed a desire to ballroom dance."

"But I thought this was going to be an opportunity for you to get out alone," he reminded me. "Remember that whole 'I've lost my identity' speech you gave me a few weeks ago? Well here's that opportunity. You do enough with the kids. It would be good for you to have something that's yours and yours alone."

It made sense. I was craving more time to myself. It would be good for me, and for my family.

I thought it over for the next few weeks. I even ran it by my sister one night on the phone.

"Well, take her if you want to."

"Well, that's the thing...I don't know if I want to. I've been wanting some time to myself for 13 years, and this might be the perfect opportunity."

"Then don't take her."

"You're not being incredibly helpful, you know."

"Well, what do you want me to say? Neither choice seems to make you happy."

"True. It's just that in a few years she won't even want to be seen with me in public, much less ballroom dancing with her own mother...."

Then it hit me. She was growing up so fast—this might be my last chance for a long time to really connect with her.

A week later I sent in my registration form for Ballroom Dancing 101, complete with tuition payment for two.

What I have decided is that some of the time it's okay to not have an identity. That now and then, it's all right to take your daughter to a ballroom dance class. It's okay even if you happen to have the only female-female partnership, one being under the age of 14.

What I have decided is that some of the time, you parent, because the parent is who you are.

On the other hand, when it's dark and late, and no one has the flu, and no one has a field trip the next day she forgot to tell you about and you're not running out at midnight to buy her a juice box to take for lunch, and you're not finishing up a miniature replica of the Roman Forum that's due tomorrow, and none of the planets are out of alignment...that's a nice time to think about reestablishing some identity.

Individual identity is important, yes. But until our children have, let's say, gotten past the age of 25 or so, their identity is our identity. And that's most likely not a crisis, but more probably the natural order of things.

Myth:
I Will Keep Them Safe at Any Cost

Chapter thirteen

Bunk Beds

For all the safety measures we take when the children are young, one purchase in a great many households amazes me. We did it. We walked into the showroom and glanced at the selection of beds, and settled (for practical reasons) on buying bunk beds. Since my two younger daughters share a room, we assumed this would be a healthy decision. What were we thinking? I really can't tell you. It was sort of like making a purchase in the pet store...you just don't know what you're getting yourself into.

Do you remember when the children were babies, and they were just on the edge of mobility? Do you remember what you spent the next few weeks doing to your home? You baby-proofed it...remember? You put latches on all your kitchen cabinets. You stuck little plastic covers into all the outlets. You bought vinyl or foam rubber to go around all the sharp corners. You gated off any and all stairways. You moved all your cleaning supplies up to a cabinet *you* couldn't even reach. You removed all extension cords, packed away all your glass, threw away anything smaller than four inches wide, got toilet latches so your kids wouldn't drown headfirst, and replaced your mini-blinds with safer, uncorded window shades. Your house became a safe-haven. A place where the children could roam free.

What happens between those years and the time when you think bringing a six-foot high bed into your home is a good idea, I will never know.

The first night after we set up the bed, my girls were so excited they could barely sleep. They had decided that my youngest would get the bottom bunk (which by the way was a double bed), and my middle daughter would sleep on the twin-size top bunk. We said goodnight to the girls, and smiled on our way downstairs when we heard them giggling about how much fun their new beds were. This joy, beautiful as it was, lasted approximately eight minutes. The first incident occurred when my middle daughter needed to use the bathroom. To save herself time, she slid down the side of the bed and landed on her sister's arm in the process. We ran upstairs to see what the crying was about, and had to give our first of many bunk-bed speeches.

"Honey, do you see the convenient ladder that has been built in to your bunk beds? Clever, isn't it? Its function is to provide a way down, one that doesn't require you wounding your sister. Do you understand?"

"Yeah, but Mom, the ladder hurts my feet. Plus it's metal, so it's cold."

"Well, then, wear thick socks to bed, Honey."

We had two more speeches to give that first night: for the bottom bunk, we gave the "when you kick the bottom of your sister's bed, it's annoying" speech. For the top bunk, we gave the "dropping heavy books from that height can break things, not to mention it scares Mommy" speech.

The rest of the week consisted of two falls out of bed in the middle of the night, one fight over whose half of the bed was cooler, one "no fair" contest when my middle daughter got to hang pictures above her bed and my youngest only had a mattress to stare at, and one more "no fair" contest when one of the kids' friends came over and pointed out that the bottom bunk was way bigger than the top.

However, until the second week started, I'd say all and all, everything was fine. At the beginning of the second week, my kids discovered that for all the fighting that had occurred over the bed the week previous, one thing remained true about a set of bunk beds. They make a fabulous makeshift jungle gym.

I am downstairs, in the kitchen washing dishes, when I

hear an enormous thud, that literally knocks my kitchen light out. I go dashing upstairs to find three blankets, four pillows, and 37 stuffed animals piled on the floor, and my two children poised on the edge of the top bunk ready to fly.

"What are you two doing?"

"We're playing, Mom! We finally figured out what to do with the bunk beds!"

In my head I am contemplating why two beds connected with a ladder should require "figuring out," when my youngest leaps six feet in the air, screaming "YAHOO!" and lands on her back, shooting stuffed animals across the room.

"WAIT! STOP!"

The children look at me confused.

"Listen, girls, the bunk beds are supposed to be for sleeping, not for bungee jumping, okay?"

More confused looks.

"Girls, you can't jump from that height and not break something, okay?"

My middle looks at me as if she understands, and says, "Oh, don't worry, Mom, we moved everything that might break." She points to the closet, where they have piled up all the things that were on their dressers.

"No, Honey, that's not what I mean. I mean break something in you. You know, like bones? It's not safe to be jumping off like that. I don't want to see you hurt."

"Well, you don't have to watch then, Mom."

I could tell, as usual, they were missing my point. As I

am sighing, my middle daughter screams, and leaps onto the blanket pile laughing.

"HONEY! I told you to stop! You're going to end up at the emergency room!"

Both my girls look at me. Their faces fall. They now realize that I mean it, that I actually want them to quit their fun. My middle daughter looks at me sad-faced. My youngest begins to cry. So I walk over and sit down to try to explain to them why I want them to stop.

"Girls, it's just that I love you so much, and I don't ever want anything to happen to you."

Back to the confused looks.

"You see, I'm your mom, and I want to keep you safe."

Bewilderment.

"It's like this. God gave me you guys as a gift, and it's my responsibility to take care of you, and make sure that you're always okay."

Pleading looks.

"But we *are* okay, Mom! We won't get hurt! We promise!"

"But, Sweetie, that's not something within your power to promise. Of course you won't try to get hurt, but you could get hurt anyway."

My youngest looks at me very seriously and offers some wisdom.

"But, Mommy, I could get hurt on my bike, and you let me ride that every day."

I am speechless. There is no proper response to her amazing tidbit of logic. She could get hurt on her bike at any time. The motherly fear seizes me for a moment, and I contemplate taking her bike away, but then I realize she's right. Protecting them, and letting them have fun at the same time, is a very taut and narrow tightrope to walk.

Suddenly I think of a story I had heard while watching the Winter X Games one year. There was a young man whose parents had gone out of town for the weekend. This young man decided to drag his bed mattress downstairs and out the front door to his yard. He placed the mattress close to the house, and then went back upstairs, climbed out on his roof, and leapt off the roof and landed on the mattress. If I remember correctly, his parents eventually came home in time to witness their son attempting to leap to his most certain death. Only for some odd reason, they didn't quite see it that way. They let the boy continue his skydiving act, and eventually this boy became an excellent ski jumper in the Winter X Games.

As I am sitting next to my children considering this story, I decide that perhaps leaping from the top bunk is not as crazy as it first seemed. I mean they had, in fact, taken several precautionary measures. They had moved all breakables. They had an excellent landing site set up. They were even going one at a time, so no one would get crushed. With some misgivings, I decided to swallow my parental urges to keep them safe at all costs and let them have their fun.

Of course before I left the room, I remade their landing site into a tower consisting of the mattress from the bottom bunk, two additional blankets, and all the pillows and stuffed animals I could locate. They were so happy that they both hugged me as I left.

"Be safe!" I called back to them, and they promised they would be.

My oldest daughter was downstairs when I came down, and asked me what all the noise was.

"Your sisters have decided that the bunk beds make an excellent launch pad."

"You mean they are jumping off them?"

"Yes."

"And you're letting them?"

"Yes, why?"

"I can't believe you! When I was their age you would've freaked out if I had done that!"

She's right. I probably would have.

"Well, you were my first, and I was terrified that you would get hurt."

She fires a disgusted look at me.

"Oh, great! So what does that mean? *I was like your guinea pig child?*"

Thinking that was a good way to put it, I sort of agreed. "See, Honey, parents learn to be parents by trial and error sometimes. Maybe I should've let you do more, I don't know. Maybe I should let your sisters do less, I don't know that either. Sometimes it's really hard to be a parent."

"Yeah, well, you should try being a kid!"

Before she walked away, I would like to have explained to her that I did try being a kid, and I made it through.

I spent the afternoon cringing at each thud, and smiling at each laugh. No one actually ended up getting hurt, and they had a great time to boot. However, that evening my youngest wiped out on her bike and ripped up her elbow and knee pretty badly. She kissed me after I patched her up and sent her back outside. I watched her get right back on her bike and she asked me if I wanted to see a trick.

My first response was to yell, "No! You just got hurt and you're going to try a trick? Just ride safely! Or better yet, get off the bike and come sit with me."

I am happy to report that all I really said was, "Sure!" I am happier to report that my youngest daughter rides beautifully with both feet up on the handlebars.

The girls have had their bunk beds now for almost two years. The beds continue to cause fights at least once a week, but the one thing both girls can still agree on, is how great it feels to stand six feet off the ground and soar into a pile of blankets and stuffed animals.

Keep soaring, girls! Keep soaring....

Myth:
What's One More?

Chapter fourteen

Four Walls, Three Kids, Two Arms

Three is an unlucky number. It's just a fact, at least where children are concerned. It's not the actual children that are the problem, however; it's simply the lack of arms. When the first one comes along you have two free arms. You can give big hugs. You can swing her around in the air. You can pick her up, and still manage to dust or cook or answer a phone.

Along comes your second child. You now have one arm full with a baby, but yet are able to hold hands with your oldest, who (with any luck) can walk by now. If necessary, you start to ignore knocks at the door, or the ring of the phone because you now have both hands full. Your house slowly becomes an allergy nightmare due to the piles of dust everywhere. Laundry gets a little out of control, and dishes pile up, but all in all it's okay. You still have enough arms for the children, so all is well.

Enter the third child.

Suddenly, without warning, what seemed utterly possible while you were pregnant becomes the biggest challenge of your life. How were you to know what a third child would mean? After all, you already have two. What's one more?

So far, how to grow another arm is a question that science has not been able to answer. That weekly grocery-shopping trip, where one child would sit up front while you piled groceries on top of the second sitting in the back until they claimed they were frozen, becomes unthinkable. Those carts are really not that big when it comes down to it, and if you let the oldest one walk you run the risk of losing him in the toy aisle. You try for a while to push a two-hundred pound cart with one hand while holding a small hand with the other, while pondering the effects of frozen vegetables on a one-year old's skin, but somehow that well-planned system you had worked out slowly turns to dust...just like your home.

So you break down and purchase the most back-breaking appliance known to humankind: the baby carrier. Now when exiting the car at the grocery store you (1) strap the baby to your front, (2) carry an infant seat with one hand while you safely (3) hold the oldest's hand in the parking lot. Collectively, you weigh a ton, and you will never be able to wear a shirt that buttons up the front again for fear of it flying open every time you adjust the baby. You have so much adrenaline churning you could probably bungee jump. But who cares? You are so proud! You have solved the grocery store dilemma. The only issue involves not dropping the baby head-first on the tile when you have to reach for something on the bottom shelf. But that is an issue easily resolved with some practice at home with a baby doll. You are a grocery store genius, and you start to think three may be quite manageable. You laugh at yourself for even thinking otherwise.

That is, until you decide to venture some place where they don't have carts.

Like the mall, for instance. This trip happens only once. After it is over and you could enter yourself in the strongman competition from all the carrying you just did, you break down and buy a double stroller. You now maneuver ten times slower than everyone else; You have to cross fifty miles to get to an elevator because escalators and stairs are obviously out of the question; You upset people intensely in the elevator because you take up 7/8ths of the elevator space; You have to listen to your oldest complain about how unfair it is that she has to walk; and when you finally leave, people honk at you for taking up too much space in the parking lot while journeying toward your car.

Also, forget any trunk space for your purchases. The entire cavity is filled with a double stroller. Still, you are proud! You were able to successfully shop and get out of the house for a while, with only the incident in the candy store when your oldest wandered off to introduce herself to Mr. Peanut. But really it was only for 30 seconds, and a guy dressed like Mr. Peanut is not going to get anywhere fast. So you count heads in the car and smile.

You have conquered yet another public place, and are quite pleased with yourself. That is, until you decide to go some place where you can't take strollers or carts.

I decided one Friday that it was time for a family outing. My oldest, who was five at the time, had been begging for some time to go somewhere that didn't involve groceries or clothes. Since an aquarium had just been built within fifty miles of our home, I thought it would be a nice change of scenery to go see the fish. After all, my oldest was getting a little stir crazy, and while infants don’t mind being home all the time, kids do. I called the aquarium that morning to see what their hours were and spoke to an employee.

"Nine a.m. to eight p.m."

"Okay. Thank you."

"Oh, and no flash photography is permitted."

“That’s okay. I haven't owned a camera since my oldest threw it straight up in the air after the fireworks frightened her on July Fourth two years ago."

"Oh, and no strollers."

Silence on my end of the line.

"What do you mean, no strollers?"

"We ask that people not bring strollers into the building, since the rooms are small, and very crowded."

"But, sir, I have two children under the age of walking. That's going to make things difficult."

"Well, a lot of folks use those front pack carriers. Do you have one of them?"

"Well, yes, but I think one of the children might resent being sandwiched behind the other one, not to mention what that would do to my back."

There was a long pause on the other line while the gentleman was trying to decide if I was attempting to be a wiseguy or a comedian.

"I'm sorry, miss. Those are the rules. Perhaps you could bring a friend with you to help."

I grudgingly hung up the phone. Our outing would have to wait until the next day when my husband wasn't working. Apparently, there were places I could not conquer alone. I told my oldest our trip would have to wait. She started to cry.

“Honey, it’s just one day. We can ask Daddy to go tomorrow.”

My oldest stops crying, and gives me a hopeful look. “You can do it, Mommy! I’ll help you. I promise!”

I don't know whether it was my ego that took over then, or the sweet look on her face, but somehow I decided that maybe we could still go. I started to brainstorm.

At the store where I had purchased the infant front pack, I had seen an infant backpack. I wondered if the straps would intertwine, or if I could actually wear one child on my front, and one on my back. Just the brilliance of how balanced I would be, made me wonder if it was possible. Maybe even good for my posture? That's it, I decided. I will go to the store, purchase a backpack, and head for the aquarium. I was not going to be thwarted. After all I had conquered malls and supermarkets; I had taken the kids to see relatives who actually owned glass knick-knacks that weren't glued together. What could be scarier?

So after a quick stop at the store, we were off to the aquarium. Strollers or no strollers, we were going in.

Now, did I fail to mention that while trying on the backpack at the store, I didn't actually place the baby in it? Also, I failed to realize that while placing a baby in a front pack on your own is fairly simple, reaching around behind your own back and securing a child is an entirely different matter. So when we finally arrived at the aquarium, and I became aware of the conundrum I was facing, my resolve began to fade.

After my oldest tried several times to slide the baby into the pack on my back, I decided to take a different approach. First, I put my middle daughter in the pack, lay down on the back seat, and without crushing her, successfully strapped her in. This took over ten minutes, a lot of kicks in the head, attracted a great many curious bystanders, but we finally accomplished it.

To get out of the back seat, however, I had to roll over and crawl out on all fours. I then proceeded to attach my littlest to my front, grab my oldest's hand, and stumble toward the ticket window.

"See, Mommy, I told you we could do it!"

I looked down and smiled. With tickets in hand we headed toward the door, and it was then that I realized how truly wide I was. Having two bodies strapped to you makes it very difficult to turn a turnstile, and even harder to navigate a doorframe. I barely squeezed through without knocking someone's head against the glass, but we had done it. We were in!

After a few minutes of fighting through crowds while literally needing at least four feet of width to get through, my resolve was again weakening. After an hour of not sitting down for fear of squishing someone, I was starting to question my own judgment. After two hours, and the loss of feeling in my shoulders, I proclaimed myself an idiot. After the funniest trip ever to the bathroom, and a strong odor of dirty diaper wafting behind me every time I moved, I decided enough was enough. I had to call it quits, or be in traction for the next three months.

Since there was physically no way of getting my middle daughter off my back without the aid of a backseat to lie down on, I announced to my oldest that it was time to go. She pouted all the way to the car.

"I wish we could stay longer."

"I'm sorry, but Mommy's fingers are turning purple and the straps on these things have produced a reverse tan line that may never fade. We'll try it another time, Honey."

After untangling the straps, finally putting all those yoga moves I learned while pregnant to good use, changing diapers, and feeding bottles, the feeling returned to my arms…at least enough to drive.

That night as I related the story to my husband, he said what I knew he'd say.

"You should've waited for me. We could've gone together."

"I know. It's just she looked at me with those eyes and gave me her little vote of confidence, and somehow I felt that it was possible. Plus, four walls, three kids and not enough arms can sometimes get to you. Of course now I realize that four walls, three kids and no feeling in my arms is worse, so I don't think I will attempt that again any time soon."

But anyone who's a mother knows that sooner or later we all break down and try the aquarium trip again. Maybe it's not the aquarium this time, maybe it's the beach, or the zoo, or a museum. But wherever it is, it's the same story...little pleading eyes and not enough arms. But we do it anyway, because it's the same as childbirth. If you (truly) remembered how awful it is you would have never done it a second and third time. But with time those painful recollections fade and all you have are good memories to replace them. A few weeks later while looking at a book about sharks, my oldest brought up our trip to the aquarium. She now remembered it quite fondly.

"See, Mom, I said you could do it!"

I smiled when she said that. Who would have thought that a five-year-old's vote of confidence would mean so much?

I guess for every mom there will be many more aquariums to stumble around, many more malls to explore, many more stops along the child-rearing trail. We know some of these adventures will be hard and backbreaking, many will be unrewarding, and a few will be downright foolish.

But with a little vote of encouragement from our child-adventurers, a touch of amnesia to soften the reality... and most important, a pair of big puppy dog eyes to tug at our hearts, I'm sure we will conquer the challenges of the next expedition.

Myth:
I Will Know My Limits

Chapter fifteen

The Colonial Hero

Sooner or later every parent breaks down and volunteers. It may be a class party, or a field trip. It may be coaching your child's little league team, or being a den mother. Whatever it is, you usually find out at some point that you've gotten in over your head. Like when you volunteer to cover for your friend's cafeteria duty, and find out later that you've now been penciled in to the cafeteria schedule every Tuesday for the balance of the school year. Or when running a booth at the school fair turns into your being in charge of organizing, distributing and overseeing all publicity involved in the event.

Somehow, once you sign up for something, you become

a target on some sort of *Underground Volunteer Hit List*. "The Sopranos" aren't as organized as the PTA and school board. When it comes down to it though, the PTA and school are not the real problem when you volunteer. It's your child that becomes the main concern. You want the class trip, or the sport they're in, or the Valentine's social to be fun for them. The best type of memory they can possibly be part of.

A few years back my oldest asked me to volunteer to help out at her school's Colonial Days. In fifth grade her school studied colonial times, and all the different ways of life and practices used back then. My daughter had been assigned to the colonial kitchen booth, and she, along with her group, was supposed to study all the customs, tools and inner workings of a colonial kitchen. She was to dress in colonial garments, find colonial kitchen supplies, and work up a speech pertaining to colonial kitchens. The children from all the other grades were then brought to the fifth grade pod, and allowed to roam around different booths and learn all things colonial. I was to be in charge of my daughter's group. Getting it organized was to be my first mission.

I thought it sounded like a fun idea at that time, and

quickly signed the sheet that was sent home, saying that I would help. Major mistake.

We had three weeks to gather the necessary clothing and kitchen items, do the research, and get ready for the presentation. My daughter started her research and soon found that in her mind, colonial times were rather boring. Even worse, colonial kitchens were the most boring subject of all, and she was upset to have been assigned to this booth in the first place.

"The only cool booths are crime & punishment, and apothecary. All I get to say is 'In a colonial kitchen they cooked over an open fire.' I mean, how boring is that! At least the apothecary group gets to bring in live leeches. Nobody's even gonna come to our booth, cause it's too boring!"

As mothers usually do, I tried to start with a pep talk.

"That's not true, Honey. I'm sure your booth will be very interesting."

"Yeah? Name one interesting thing in all the kitchen research we've done!"

I should have prepared for this question ahead of time. I should have picked out at least one fascinating fact about colonial kitchens, and cataloged it for when I had to defend my position. The problem was that for all the reading up on colonial times we had done, there really weren't that many interesting points to make. She was right. To most people, kitchens just aren't that interesting at any point in history.

So instead of brilliantly avoiding disaster, I fumbled for

whatever I could.

"Well there's...I mean, at least the tools...there is the..."

Nothing. I came up with nothing.

"You see!" she said and started to cry.

"It is the worst topic. Nobody's even going to come to our booth."

Feeling sorry for her, I said the only thing that came into my mind.

"There's bread."

She looked up at me as if I had lost my mind and said,

"What?"

"There's bread. In colonial times they made their own bread, right?"

"Yeah...and?"

"Well, maybe we could make our own bread."

"Well, that's great for home, Mom, but I don't think bringing in a loaf of homemade bread and showing it around is really going to be that fascinating."

She was right. Just a loaf of bread sitting there...that was not going to dazzle the crowd. I had to think fast, if I was going to save myself.

"Okay, you're right, but what if we gave out samples of bread? Kids love to eat, right? They'll be sure to come to a booth with free food, won't they?

My daughter's face brightened.

"You're right! In the morning, everyone will be hungry because they won't have eaten lunch, and everyone in the afternoon will be hungry 'cause they already ate lunch hours ago. That's perfect, Mom. Now everyone will come!"

I was so excited that I had solved the problem. I felt great when my daughter hugged me and thanked me for saving the day. I sat down, very pleased with my own brilliant problem-solving skills, until I really thought about what I had just done. I had just volunteered to feed 512 elementary school students bread. And not just any white bread off the shelves, I had volunteered homemade bread of which I had never made before, and furthermore, I had no idea what was even involved. My gloating soon turned to questioning, and I silently called myself a few names under my breath.

What had I been thinking?

When the kids were put to bed that night I revealed to my husband my promise to provide bread.

"I just blurted it out before I had time to think!"

"Well, Honey, I don't think you can really accomplish feeding 512 kids, so you're just going to have to tell her it won't work, and come up with a different idea."

I agreed, and planned to talk to my daughter after school the next day. She'd just have to understand. Too much bread is just too much bread.

So when my daughter arrived home from school, I sat her down to inform her of the bad news.

"Honey, remember yesterday when we talked about Colonial Days and the bread? Well I...."

"Oh yeah, Mom, I wanted to tell you...I told my group

today and they were all so excited. Then my teacher came over and asked us what we were excited about, and she said she thought the bread was a great idea! Thank you, Mom for thinking of it! You're the best!"

She hugged me and asked if she could go get a snack. I told her that was fine.

When my husband came home from work he asked me how the bread talk had gone.

"Well...not exactly how I'd planned."

"Oh, I'm sorry, Sweetie. Was she really upset?"

"Not exactly."

Apparently the look on my face spoke volumes, and my husband, having seen this face before, figured things out.

"You didn't tell her, did you?"

"I tried. It's just she told her group already, and her teacher, and everyone was so excited. I just didn't want to crush her hopes."

"Well, I don't want to have to sell the house and hire a team of bakers in order to feed other people's children, so do you have a plan B, or should I cash in my 401k now?"

I told my husband that I would set aside a 20-dollar budget for bread and that if I couldn't do it for that amount, I would break the bad news to her. We agreed. 20 dollars worth of bread. Bread that I didn't know how to make, and after a slight amount of research into the cost of soaring gas prices, bread pans, yeast, and other ingredients, I decided making it was not cost-effective. I was going to have to buy it.

So I spent the next three days calling around to different grocery stores and bakeries and asking about bread prices. I finally found two stores that put all of their yesterday's bread on special for 89 cents a loaf. I purchased a practice loaf and found that if cut correctly, each loaf could yield about 30 small wedges. I rejoiced at my ingenuity, and reveled in not having to break my daughter's heart.

After a week of calling around to everyone I know to help me put together a colonial costume, I finally stitched something suitable for both of us to wear. Then, after sitting through at least 100 practice speeches by my daughter, the day finally arrived.

Colonial Days didn't start until 9:15 a.m., which meant I would have just enough time to drop the kids at school, run to the store and buy the bread, go home and cut it into 512 pieces, and arrive on time to oversee the magic that was the colonial kitchen. I had it all planned perfectly and kissed my daughter goodbye, and told her that I'd see her soon. She smiled a huge smile and disappeared into school.

I happily drove to the store. However, the problem with having to buy "yesterday's bread" is that you have to wait until the last minute, and it never dawned on me that yesterday's bread might have been a best-seller...yesterday. So I arrived to find today's bread fully stocked, and only two loaves of yesterday's bread. I made a mental tabulation as to the cost of buying enough of today's bread at $2.89 a loaf, and realized that I would be spending a small fortune.

So I quickly bought the two loaves they had, and drove to the other store that carried yesterday's bread. When I arrived I found ten loaves of yesterday's bread which I immediately purchased, along with (don't tell my husband) four loaves of today's bread to make up the difference. Since the extra driving had eaten up a lot of time, I made a quick stop, purchased a .99 cent knife to cut the bread, then headed straight for school. I decided I would just slice and hand out the bread right there at the booth.

When I arrived at school I ran to the fifth grade pod, and began to set up my bread-cutting station. My daughter was happy to see me and I breathed a sigh of relief at having pulled the whole plan off.

A moment later, however, I was greeted with a tap on the shoulder. It was my daughter's teacher, who whispered in my ear.

"I'm sorry, but we aren't allowed to bring knives to school per our school weapons policy. I'll have to confiscate that."

I discreetly handed her the knife, which another teacher then took down to the main office. I was told I could pick it up on my way out at the end of the day. My embarrassment was the least of my concerns, however, as we now had 16 loaves of bread and no way except ripping and tearing to separate the bread into 512 pieces. The teacher offered a suggestion.

"If you take the bread down to the cafeteria, they have plastic knives down there that you could use."

I told my daughter, who was developing a worried look on her face, to hang in there. I told her I would be back as quickly as possible.

Now I don't know if you've ever tried to cut 16 loaves of French bread into 512 pieces with a plastic cafeteria knife, but I'm here to tell you it's quite a challenge. Incredibly time-consuming as well. So I decided to cut and carry back bread in shifts, so the handing out of free food could commence.

After many knives breaking, several blisters, and one band aid (yes, plastic knives can cut your fingers), I had conquered the challenge of the bread. My daughter's booth was a hit! Many kids were repeat customers, announcing that they were still hungry, so we broke many of the pieces in half quite a few times. The day went by and we were a huge success. We drove home from school that afternoon, and my daughter went on and on about how many people came to their booth. She was happy, and I had somehow managed to be the hero!

* * *

Fast-forward a few years. It is now my middle daughter's turn to study colonial times. She marches in the door after the day of booth assignments and informed me that she didn't like her topic.

"Well, what is it?"

"I was assigned to colonial fabric-making. I mean, is that the most boring topic you've ever heard of? What's cool about knitting and weaving? Nothing!"

"Oh, I'm sure it'll be fun. Your sister was upset when she got her topic too, but it turned out to be a great day."

"Yeah, that's 'cause she got colonial kitchen! Colonial kitchen's cool. She got to hand out free bread, and everyone loved it."

I secretly smiled and remember the bread idea and all the trouble that followed. The bottom line, though, is my oldest recalls the day fondly, and I had something to do with that.

I decide to pull another brilliant idea out of my "I Have No Idea How This Is Going to Work, but it Sounds Good" Hat.

"You know, they used to weave on looms."

"Yeah...and?"

"Well, maybe we could make a big loom, and each of the kids who comes to your booth could weave one part of a blanket or something. You could put up a LEARN TO WEAVE sign."

My daughter's eyes sparkled.

"Yeah, kids would like that! Something they could participate in. That's a good idea, Mom!"

Once again I marveled at my own brilliance and my ability to save the day. My only problem now is how in the world am I going to figure out how to build a loom, gather materials, then learn to weave in the next three weeks, all on a budget of under twenty dollars.

I wonder. Do you think being a bona fide colonial hero was as difficult in colonial times as it is today?

Myth:
Honesty Is the Best Policy

Chapter sixteen

Ugly Feet and Poignant Logic

"I hate my hair. And I can't stand my nose...oh, and I have the grossest looking feet of anyone in my whole gym class!"

"Honey you look beautiful."

"You have to say that, you're my mom!"

True. I am her mom, and by all accounts that does mean I have to say that.

"Well then, ask a neutral party."

"Like who?"

"I don't know...ask one of your friends."

"They won't tell me either. They'll say I look fine."

"Then ask an enemy."

"Oh, forget it...."

This is the moment when I try to turn this situation into yet another opportunity for growth.

"Honey, don't you think it's nice that you have so many people who care about you so much they wouldn't say anything unkind to you and hurt your feelings?"

"Great! So everyone does hate my feet—they just won't say it!"

My middle daughter storms off, in order to bathe in self-pity. I sit down at the table to try to re-work my speech, so when my youngest pulls the same thing on me in a few years, I will promote less of a need for therapy when she's an adult.

Over the years I have perfected certain speeches. However, the perfection of the speech may not matter if it falls on deaf ears: in other words, any child over the age of five. I have become adept at giving the *"Starving Children in Africa"* speech, complete with the comeback for the classic *"Then Send Them My Dinner"* response. I tell them that it would be an insult to send anyone rotten, half-eaten food, and that the postal service would never stand for the odor it would produce. If I'm feeling extra clever, I throw in the "*If You Are Really Concerned We Can Save Your Allowance and Send It to Africa*" challenge.

I have perfected the speech on monsters not being real. If that doesn't seem to work, I have the back-up reference of several movies that have "nice" monsters in them.

I have given the *"Boy Who Cried Wolf"* fable more

meaning over the years than I'm sure was ever intended, including how people will not only think you're fooling them, but will not like you in the process and how that would not make your mother proud.

I have given the reverse *"Chicken Little"* speech, where indeed the sky could fall at any time, BUT if you spend all your time worrying and waiting you'll miss out on all the good things.

I have given the "if your friends jump off a bridge...", the "even if he can't find his puppy, he's still a stranger...", and the "sticks and stones hurt, but so do words" speech. I have quoted fairy tales, fables, poems, books, movies and whatever other paraphernalia that I think will convey my point. I should earn the wage of a professional speech-giver by now. I am the valedictorian of our home. I should be hired out for commencements.

The only problem with speech-giving in my house is that my kids (like most, I guess) think they know more than I do. This is a gradual process which has occurred over the course of many years of speech-giving. One day, they look at you as if you are insane and proclaim, "you already told me that a million times."

Last week, my oldest was the recipient of the "*Elves Do Not Sneak in at Night and Do the Laundry, So Please Make Sure Things Get into the Hamper—It's Only Fair....*" speech.

She came out with the now infamous reply.

"Mom, you've already told me this."

"Well, then, I expect you would be so sick of hearing it that you'd do it just to shut me up."

"I do pick it up sometimes. It's just I can't be perfect, you know."

"Nobody is asking you to be perfect, Honey. I just want you to do normal things expected of a thirteen-year-old."

"So, what? Now I'm not normal?"

"I didn't say that. I am simply asking you to pick up your dirty clothes."

"Fine. I'll try to be your version of normal then...."

Pointless. The entire conversation was pointless, as are many of the speeches I have given recently. By the way, if this keeps up I am going to encourage my oldest to attend a performing school of the arts. She definitely has a flair for the dramatic.

My speech giving years are, I'm sure, far from over, so as of late I have tried to adopt shorter, slightly more sarcastic ways of getting my point across. I have decided I am not only wasting air, but precious mental energy that could be used in more productive ways. So when my middle daughter came back downstairs to show me her feet, and prove her "see, they are disgusting" point, I just stared.

"Well, I guess you're lucky someone invented socks then."

"So you do think they're ugly!"

"No."

"Then why did you say that?"

"Because if I say they're beautiful, you'll just say that I'm your mom and I HAVE to say that."

I rendered her speechless with my poignant logic. At least for all of three seconds.

"Aaahh Ha! So you would say they're fine just cause you're my mom!"

That's when I gave up. Because it just isn't worth it.

"Yes. You're right. I will always say you're beautiful no matter what. If you are in a car accident, and you are unrecognizable, I will still walk into your hospital room and hug you and say you're beautiful. Is that so wrong? Don't look to me for a brutally honest answer, because as your mother I am incapable of giving one. Okay? I love you too much. Most people would pay good money for that kind of love!"

That speech was the first in many years that had any impact. But I didn't know it had any, and would never have known, if I hadn't stumbled across my daughter playing house with her friend a few days later. I walked past her room and listened in the slightly opened door and heard this...

"No, let's pretend that we're teenagers and we're going to the prom."

"How about we're homeless people and someone takes us in?"

My daughter replied, "How about I'm your mom, and the house catches on fire and you go to the hospital. And when I walk in I hug you, and I keep telling you that you're beautiful even though none of the nurses will let you see a mirror!"

"Okay!"

They played out that scenario until dinner time. While I was cooking, I decided that all the speeches given DO have a place in our house, that somehow in their own way, when the time comes, my kids will use what I teach them. They may not fully understand *"The Fisherman and His Wife"* now, but someday, somewhere, they will learn to be content with what they have. Whether it be ugly feet, dirty laundry, or a speech-making mom that loves them so much she might (on rare occasions) be less than completely honest.

Addendum:
Should your child pull out the "*What About Man-Eating Sharks*?" during the "*There Are No Monsters*" speech, simply explain to them that man-eating sharks, while real, live in the ocean, and could never get into her bedroom at night and devour her. However, be prepared on your next vacation at the seashore to have your child spend one whole day out of the water.

Addendum Number Two:
Should one of your children then tease you by saying there is one real monster, and that her name is "Mom on Cleaning Day", consider feeding her to the sharks next time you're at the seashore.

Myth:
I Will Be Appreciated in Sickness and in Health

Chapter seventeen

When Children Fall Ill

My oldest came downstairs one morning looking pale. She said she wasn't feeling well. I took her temperature, and indeed she had a fever. 100.3. I sent her back to bed, after giving her medicine and a glass of water, and asking if she needed anything.

"No. I guess not...Well, I guess I could eat some Jell-O and crackers. I'm really hungry."

Even though we had no Jell-O or crackers in the house, I told her I would run out to the store and get some. No problem. She's sick. I'll humor her.

So she shuffles up to her room to rest, and I decide the situation is serious enough that I will not go into work today.

Instead, I head over to the grocery store. The store is sold out of ready-made Jell-O, so I have to buy it from the box. I don't remember which crackers she likes, so I buy an assortment. Home I go, to find my oldest lying on the sofa, looking at me.

"What took you so long?"

I assume it's the fever talking, so I apologize, and get straight to boiling the water for Jell-O. I then bring in four different cracker boxes for her to choose from.

"I don't think I want crackers anymore. I want toast instead."

"Oh, okay, Sweetie. I'll make some right now."

"I'm thirsty too. Do we have any ginger ale? And can you shake the fizz out for me?"

I smile and pat her head.

"Whatever you need, Sweetie. I'm really sorry you don't feel well."

I go to the kitchen to discover that the bread is stale, and of course, we have no ginger ale left.

"Honey, we don't have either. Can I get you something else?"

After listening to a huff and a sigh, I break down and run back to the grocery store, and purchase the soda and a loaf of bread. I hurry out of the checkout line, and get home in record time.

"What took you so long? I haven't eaten anything yet, and my stomach is starting to hurt."

I apologize again, and set straight to the kitchen to

shake the fizz out, and make the toast.

"Mom? Can you make me jelly toast, and not cinnamon toast?"

"Of course, Honey!" I shout back.

I open the refrigerator to find...you guessed it...an empty jar of jelly.

"Honey, someone ate all the jelly."

"WHAT! Oh my gosh! You mean I'm gonna have to wait like another whole hour while you run out and get some?"

I put my shoes back on and get back in the car. By this time, one of the cashiers at the store is eyeing me suspiciously, so I decide that I'm going to be smart and buy anything and everything I might ever need to feed this child. However, I also decide that I must do it in record time, to be sure that my poor, sick daughter won't have to starve to death for much longer. So I race through the grocery store dropping anything that looks edible into my cart, and speed through the checkout, and I run to the car, and I load in the bags as fast as I can, and race home.

When I get there, my daughter is eating the crackers from the first trip to the store, and proclaims that it took me so long that she couldn't wait any longer. I go to make her toast, but she tells me she's full now.

Because you're a mother, this is the way you treat children when they contract some sort of illness. You bend over backwards, you encourage them to get all the rest they need, and basically, you wait on them hand and foot without a word of thanks in return.

Have you noticed it's a bit different when we moms get sick?

* * *

When Mom (God Forbid) Falls Ill

About once a year I get so sick that I can barely move. When these illnesses happen my children usually decide they miss me terribly and want to bond. Recently, I had pneumonia, and anyone who's had pneumonia knows that you can barely move your left pinky, much less speak in coherent sentences. At the depths of this mental and physical state is when my youngest daughter decided that she and I needed to spend some quality time together. So while lying in bed, trying to find my mouth in order to feed myself, my youngest burst into my room.

"Mommy, can you quiz me on my math homework?"

(Gurgle, cough, wheeze) "Why, honey? (sputter) Do you have a test?" (choke)

"No. I just want to practice."

(Nose blowing) "Well, Mommy's not feeling too good (deep breath). Could we do this when I'm (another deep breath)... better?"

"I guess so."

She leaves. I think I have won the battle. And I have. Except that I didn't know the battle was just a precursor to the coming war.

Five minutes later, a tiny head peeks in my room door.

"Mommy?"

(Inhale, gurgling breath) "Yes?"

"Since you're not feeling good, I'll make dinner tonight."

"Oh, thank you (pant) except, (stammer) you're only eight years old, Honey... (recovery time)...and you can't cook yet." (series of convulsive coughs)

"I don't have to cook mommy. I can make a cold dinner. Maybe sandwiches?"

"That sounds nice." (gasp)

Door shuts, and I close my eyes. I am on the threshold of sleep, when...

"Mommy?"

One eye opens.

(burble) "Yes?"

"What kind of sandwiches should I make?"

"How about peanut butter and (stifle violent obstruction of lungs)...jelly?"

"Okay."

Door shuts. I close my eyes, feeling almost delirious from the talking and exertion, when...

"Mommy?"

"What! (speaking above a whisper sends me into a sequence of noises that I wasn't aware the human body could make)

"Mommy, are you okay?"

"No, Honey. Mommy's not... (crackle)...okay."

"I'm sorry, but I can't find the peanut butter."

"Check your sister's room." (choke, seizure)

Door shuts. I lie in raspy anticipation, but I hear no other noise. A tear of joy silently glides down my cheek as I close my eyes.

"Mommy?"

"Okay! That's it! (bubble, wheeze) Honey, Mommy's really sick! (pant, spit) and I need to sleep!" (suffocate, gasp)

"Oh, I'm sorry Mommy. I won't bug you anymore. I'll go now."

"Thank you." (asthmatic convulsions, epilepsy)

The door closes, and somewhere deep-down I feel bad for yelling. But it's way deep down, and in the end it's not even that bad. My head sinks deep into my stack of pillows, propped so as not to obstruct my airway. I proceed to the remainder of a box of tissues to clear my nose, wipe the tears of frustration from my eyes, and bring my breathing back into the acceptable range. My eyes start to close, and my mind relaxes, and I fall into a slumber.

Looking back on it, it was the best four minutes I've ever had.

"Mommy?"

(no noise except gurgling from my lungs)

"Mommy?"

(still no noise, but face now contorted into a pleading

expression)

"Oh, Mommy (playful)...I made you a sandwich. (smile) It's only jelly, cause the peanut butter was in the laundry closet, and it smelled like socks, but maybe it'll help you feel better. Did you have a nice nap?"

Surrender. It was all that was left. I sat up. Took the sandwich. Made noises that sounded like a jet taxiing down the runway, and ate. I washed it down with a glass of lukewarm water (also provided for my enjoyment) and lay back down.

"Do you want anything else Mommy?"

I decided that it was pointless. Why fight it? God distinctly created daytime so parents would know when they were NOT allowed to lie down. Sick or not sick, the sun was still up, and the rules are never going to change just for me. However, there was nothing in the rules that said I couldn't at least try to be clever.

"Yes. (hiss) There is something I would like."

"There is? (excitement) What do you want, Mommy? Anything! Just name it."

"I want you to stay in here...(suck in air) and watch... (stifle rumbling) the news with...(murmur) me."

"Oh. (a little less excited) Okay."

She sits down on the edge of my bed, and I turn on *CNN Headline News*. It only takes three minutes. Shorter than I expected.

"Mommy?"

"(gasp, sputter, choke, wheeze)

"Yes?" (pant, crackle, spit)"

"Would you mind if I went out to play? I don't really like the news."

Tears of joy flow freely now, and I can barely contain the ecstasy in my heart. But for the sake of the charade, I must.

"Yeah, that's okay (whistling through my chest). But what do you think? Maybe we could watch (catch breath) *60 Minutes* later?" (sputter)

Well, I am happy to report that after some strong antibiotics, I eventually recovered. I am happier to report that my reverse psychology worked. My youngest never did report back that night. However, my middle daughter stopped in to get me to sign a field trip permission form, and my oldest came to ask if I could drive one way to the movies this weekend. Even my husband was nice enough to show up for a visit, to ask where I had put the Phillips head screwdriver.

A few days after my recovery, my youngest came over and sat on my lap and told me that she had missed me while I was sick. I wanted to break out in uncontrollable laughter. Missed me? I don't think I've ever seen my family so often as I did that week in bed. In the end I just told her I had missed her too, and left it at that.

There's a saying about absence making the heart grow fonder. Just a suggestion to families everywhere.... This statement indeed does ring true, however, defining the word absence is the key to having the theory really work.

My family has always been bad at researching definitions. Every time I ask them to look up a word, such as "absence," someone has misplaced the dictionary, perhaps along with the peanut butter in the laundry closet, or under a bed after a language arts assignment, or even more bizarre, on the bookshelf in the den where we would never think to look.

Myth:
I Will Know What My Children Are up to at All Times

Chapter eighteen

Stuff

The other day I asked my middle daughter to take out the trash for me.

"How much?" she asked.

"Oh, just one bag."

"No, I mean how much would you pay me?"

I stared blankly.

"You mean money?

"Yeah. My friend gets paid a dollar a bag to take out the trash at her house."

"Honey, with the amount of trash our family makes in a day I'd have to mortgage the house to pay you."

"Yeah, but I want to earn some money."

"You mean besides that free allowance Dad and I give you every month. What could a ten-year-old possibly need extra money for?"

"Stuff."

"What kind of stuff?"

"Just *stuff*, that's all."

*   *   *

Be prepared for the times when your children need "stuff." Or "things," for that matter. Sometimes their reasons for needing "stuff" will include "none of your business," or "why do you want to know?" or even "I just do, okay?"

It appears that from the age of ten and beyond, there is a type of secret society that children must pay annual dues to. A society where all they do is acquire stuff, things, whatyamacallits, and thingamabobs. And don't think the exorbitant allowance they already receive from you will take care of it. And definitely don't think if you sit down and rationally try to discuss what things they need, you will get some sort of a straight answer out of them.

Some of the "stuff' that has allegedly been accrued over the years in our home includes: a set of walkie-talkies (necessary for our youngest fulfilling her dreams of becoming a spy), a video about having a modeling career (again something to do with elusive dreams), a bottle of extremely expensive shampoo that appeared in our shower one day (this was soon after the modeling video, and several comments in reference to "mom buying the cheap stuff"), and the list goes on and on.

I used the word *allegedly* because I can't actually prove these items are "stuff;" I just know that I was approached for money, and the "stuff" appeared shortly after the request, and I didn't purchase any of it.

I try to explain the "stuff" issue to my middle daughter.

"You know, while I appreciate you at least trying to earn the money for your "stuff," I am not handing out a dollar per bag of trash to a ten-year-old. Dad and I have a budget we try to stick to, and it doesn't include mystery items for the children in it. If you could explain to me exactly what it is you need, I'd be happy to see if it fits into our budget."

"Oh, forget it. I'll just see if I can borrow it from one of my sister's."

My daughter walks off, and I say over and over to myself, "Ten-year-olds have no access to drugs...ten-year-olds have no access to drugs…"

"Mom?"

I turn around to see my oldest standing there.

"You girls aren't on drugs are you?"

"What? No! Where did that come from? You've been watching too much TV."

"It's just you girls seem to have an unusual need for money, and you refuse to explain to me what it's for, and your sister already has walkie-talkies and...."

"Okay, Mom, calm down. You're starting to scare me. Nobody's on drugs, Mom. Okay?"

After a few minutes of me mumbling things about expensive shampoo, my daughter settles me down.

"Mom, it's okay. None of us are on drugs. I just wanted to see if I could borrow some money and lend it to my sister, that's all."

"What for?" I asked hopefully…

"Just something, that's all."

"In what world is "something" a good answer? I really don't understand this language you kids are speaking anymore. You used to see a commercial and run in and say, *'Mommy! I want the fishy game with the little rods and the magnets that pick up the fish. You know the red and blue one with that little wind up switch on the side! I wrote the 800 number down.'* Now you all just want *stuff*. I don't get it."

"Don't worry, Mom, she just wants to borrow a couple dollars, and no it's not for a fishy game, but it's not for drugs either."

Deciding that I will never be let into the secret "stuff" society, I decide it's time to give in.

"How many dollars?"

"Six."

"Okay, but if your sister ever ends up on drugs I will hold you personally responsible!"

My daughter pats my arm condescendingly and agrees to my terms. When Dad gets home later I think I hear her telling the "mom thinks we're doing drugs" story and then laughter. Personally I don't see the humor in this, so I decide that I am going to be a secret agent. I am going to find out where the six dollars went if it kills me.

So over the course of the next week I do a search of every room in the house. I check closets and under beds. I toss drawers and check for new holes dug in the yard. I make sure I get the mail every day to see if a secret package arrives, but I wind up empty-handed. Nothing seems out of place. There are no new items to be found, minus a suspicious looking doll that turns out to belong to a neighbor. I am baffled.

Where could all this "stuff" money be going? What kind of trickery is afoot? I finally give up trying to solve the case, but secretly check the children's eyes at dinner every night for extreme pupil dilation.

A few weeks go by and my middle daughter forgets to take her violin to school one day. I decide to take pity on her and take it over to the school office and drop it off, so she won't miss her lesson. Little did I know that I was about to solve the mystery of the six dollars.

The office secretary asks me who I am dropping off the violin for, and I give her my daughter's name and room number. Upon hearing her name the secretary hands me a small purple wallet, and asks me to return it to my daughter.

"Oh, did she lose it?" I ask curiously.

"No, she left it here when she dropped off her donation."

"Donation?"

"Oh yes, it was so sweet. She brought in a donation for a club we started to help out two families at our school whose children have cancer."

"Did the donation happen to be six dollars?"

"Actually there was six dollars in bills, and then a whole bunch of change. I believe it added up to ten dollars exactly, but I'd have to check."

I told the office secretary not to worry about checking, and that I'd return the wallet to my daughter. I left school that morning beaming with pride over my daughter's generosity. I decided to turn in my detective's badge that day as well. Not that someday I won't have to worry where the "stuff" money is going, and not that I won't keep communicating with the kids about the dangers of drugs. But that day, for that moment, I had nothing at all to worry about. My daughter had helped out another child in need, and didn't even want recognition for it. I couldn't have been more proud.

It turns out that her younger sister had been the one to provide all the extra change that was donated. The two of them had combined the money to make ten dollars even, because they had reasoned that it was a respectable amount.

So now when the kids approach me for money for "stuff" I give them the benefit of the doubt. Maybe ten-year-olds do need extra money sometimes. Maybe for a walkie-talkie, maybe for a package of sea monkeys or expensive shampoo. Maybe for something no more fishy than a simple fishy game. Who knows?

And maybe, just maybe, the "stuff" money your children ask for might be intended to help a person they know needs the money more than they do.

Myth:
I Will Plan Ahead—with Great Efficiency—for My Children's Future

Chapter nineteen

The Incredible Teenage Appetite

The older your children get, the better they eat. While this may sound encouraging to the mothers who have small ones who will eat nothing but Cheerios for all three meals, don't be fooled. This truth is a double-edged sword.

When my oldest was a baby, she made the decision that no baby food except strained carrots was going to enter her mouth. We tried all the varieties of baby food on the market. Every brand, every assortment, only to reach the same conclusion...if it wasn't carrots, she was going to pucker her lips, make a strange face, and spit. So, we decided that if we were actually going to sustain her long enough to see toddlerhood, we were going to feed her nothing but carrots. This seemed like a good decision at the time, but after a few weeks I noticed that our baby daughter was developing a strange coloring to her skin.

Being that she was my first child, I immediately rushed her off for a doctor's appointment. The nurse came in to check my daughter, and instantly asked what I was feeding her. I embarrassingly told her about the carrots, and she told me that too many carrots *can* actually turn the skin a faint shade of orange. I was then informed that I needed to supplement other things into my daughter's diet, or she would remain orange.

I am happy to say, that after several weeks of showering her with everything from strained peas to blueberry parfait, I was able to get her skin coloring back to normal (not green, not purple). Eventually she overcame her dislike of variety, and I was able to successfully make her into "a good little eater."

Fast-forward thirteen years...

I now have a teenager. And a teenager functions on an entirely different set of eating rules. The rules are as follows:

1. I will eat everything in the house.
2. I will invite as many other teenagers as possible into my home to partake of this gluttonous smorgasbord.
3. Refer to rules 1 and 2.

Ironic isn't it? That you can go from spending forty-nine cents a week struggling to get some kind of nourishment into your child, to taking out a home equity loan just to visit the grocery store. The biggest irony in my case is that my oldest now can't stand carrots. They are her least favorite food.

My grocery bill to feed a family of five has grown to epic proportions. I know people are always worried when they first have a baby about the cost it will add to their family. But really, the cost of diapers and formula versus the cost of laying out a meal for a herd of teenagers is nothing.

Herd? Even one teen can wipe out your grocery budget in a single afternoon.

I came home the other day, a few minutes after my daughter had gotten home from school, to find that my oldest had suddenly turned into Emeril Lagasse. My kitchen was covered in freshly cut fruit skins, assorted empty yogurt containers, half a used orange juice carton, and the blender was running top speed, full to the brim. I started checking around the kitchen to see if anyone was hiding.

"What are you doing, Mom?"

"I'm checking to see how many friends you must've brought home."

"What are you talking about? I didn't bring anyone home."

"Well, then, try to explain to me why the contents of that blender say otherwise. I am positive you couldn't be attempting to eat that all by yourself."

"I was just making a smoothie. I got the recipe from my friend at school."

"Well, perhaps your friend quadrupled the recipe when you weren't looking, since you have now used up what I considered our fruit and yogurt budget for the entire week."

To this comment, I receive a roll of the eyes.

"Mom, I'm really hungry!"

"Well you'd have to be, wouldn't you?"

Another eye-roll.

"Don't worry. I'll eat it."

My daughter then proceeded to pour herself a thirty-two ounce smoothie and carry it over to the computer.

"Can I go on the Internet for a while?"

"Yes, I guess so...." My words stop and my eyes pop when I see what else is in front of the computer. Lined up on plates, in what looks to be the "Be Our Guest" number from Disney's *Beauty and the Beast* is a feast fit for a multitude. Waiting for the smoothie are a sandwich complete with extra lunchmeat and cheese, with a pickle on the side, some crackers with peanut butter, a leftover piece of chicken from last night's dinner, a piece of half-eaten pie, and a glass of water. Still in a daze I wander over and peruse the banquet.

"What in the world...?"

"Don't worry, Mom. I said I'd eat it!"

"That's what I'm worried about. What should the rest of us eat for this week?"

I proceed to pick up the water glass and play the old Sesame Street game, "One of These Things Is Not Like the Other."

"I mean, really, the water is truly out of place here, isn't it? Why go to all the trouble of eating us out of house and home, just to finish it off with something free from the faucet?"

"Oh, it's not from the faucet. It's the spring water from the fridge."

This comment sends me over the edge, and I move into my speech about how I can't afford to run a café based in my own kitchen.

"Then why do you buy all of this in the first place?"

"Because I expected to ration it out over a reasonable period of time."

My daughter gets up and huffs. "Fine. Then I'll put something back."

She picks up the piece of chicken and sticks it back in the fridge.

"Is that better?"

Still dazed, I scramble to take a stand. I walk over and grab her glass of water.

"You already have a $20.00 smoothie to drink, so I guess you won't be needing this!"

I take a triumphant swig of water, and leave with the glass. It is possibly the saddest stand I've ever taken.

That night my daughter asks to invite a friend over after school the next day.

"Not the smoothie recipe kid, is it? I'd hate to have to buy a larger blender."

Not amused, she informs me that, no, it is indeed not

the smoothie kid.

The next day I walk in to find my daughter and her friend standing with the refrigerator door open, just staring.

"Hi, Mom. There's nothing to eat."

"Oh, that's funny. I could've sworn there was lunch-meat, and cheese, and rolls, and pie, and fruit, and yogurt, and chicken— just yesterday."

"Well where's that leftover chicken I put back then?"

"Oh, my goodness! You mean someone else in this house actually had the nerve to eat that!"

Sensing my sarcasm, she decides to drop it.

"Forget it. We're going upstairs to study instead."

As they walked up the stairs I decided I couldn't resist. "Oh, but I do have some carrots leftover, if you're really hungry!"

I heard a faint "Ha, ha, ha" from the hallway before her door closed, and I tried hard not to think about what my food bill will be in a few years, when they all have teenage appetites.

Later I discovered in the trash an empty bag of chips, two empty dip containers, two discarded juice boxes, and several candy wrappers. It seems as if these devoured snacks qualified as "nothing to eat."

Just a thought: If you are a younger parent, and your children are still babies and toddlers, forget about setting up a college fund. If you feel like you have to plan ahead, take cash and put it in containers in your kitchen cabinet, each jar labeled "food money." (Large jars, not baby food jars.)

You might not collect interest from this special fund, but when you really need it, the money will be in the right place at the right time.

Myth:
From the Birth of Your First Baby, Your Most Important Family Pictures Are Kept in an Album

Chapter twenty

Memories of the Mind

I'd be willing to bet none of us can remember the first meal mom cooked for us, or the first time she drove us to the movies. We don't remember the first time she washed our dishes, or helped us clean our rooms, or read us a story. In fact, I bet we remember very little about the mundane day-to-day events of our childhood. I don't think our brains function that way. If an event is not noteworthy, if it doesn't stand out from other events, it somehow loses significance.

One thing I love to do with my girls is reminisce. "Remember the time...?" has become one of my favorite events in our house. It somehow lends meaning and purpose to family life when you can look back and revel in all the nice times spent together, in all the memories you cannot only recall, but have actually made together. I think this is one of the reasons parents are so obsessed with picture- and video-taking, because someday in the future, you can remind your children of beautiful times together. This reminder becomes even more important when you enter the teen years, and your child no longer wants to vacation with her family, unless of course, she can bring a friend and pretend the entire time that she doesn't belong to you.

The other day, my oldest pulled out pictures from one year's family beach trip. She remembered it fondly.

"Hey mom, look at this one…remember this?"

I stepped closer to see a picture of our family in front of a boardwalk laser tag sign.

"Oh yeah, I remember, how could I ever forget that!"

A few years back we had gone on our annual girls' beach trip. Every year on our last day at the beach, we try to do something new and different, so we can end our vacation with a bang. This particular year, the girls had suggested that we all try laser tag. My daughter and I stared at the photo and had a good laugh remembering the fact that, the only other available laser tag team waiting for a showdown that day was a group of five teenage boys. When those boys had entered the waiting area and saw that their competition consisted of one sunburned mom, and three girls under the age of nine, even the best of actors would have had trouble capturing the look of horror on their faces. I'm sure you're aware that laser tag is not cheap entertainment, and these boys had probably been looking for some formidable opponents for their laser tag dollar. (Or at least a group of attractive teenage girls.) But that day, my children and I were what they got.

I considered telling the kids that maybe we should go mini-golfing. When I looked over at the kids, who were now staring up at their adversaries towering over them, I smelled their fear. I almost told the gentleman who was placing a twenty-pound vest over my head, that we had changed our minds. My oldest even whispered in my ear that "maybe we should go ask for a refund."

Now, the kids had been looking forward to this since the first night on the boardwalk when they had spotted the sign, and having been a mom for many years, I knew what would happen if we backed out. The girls would talk all the way home about how they never got to try laser tag. They would bring it up for years to come, whenever that particular year was mentioned. It would become, in the journals of their mind, nothing more than the year we did *not* try laser tag.

So I decided to give the girls a pep talk, because I was now determined this had to be done. For the sake of all future beach trip memories, we were going to give these boys a run for their money. I huddled the girls in and started with the fact that they were small, but that was a good thing because that made it easier for them to hide. I went on to say that because of their size they were also harder targets. I finished with the thought that kids are definitely more agile, and so they should dive behind things whenever necessary. I think I may have gone overboard though, because when the bell rang to start play, my middle daughter looked up at a boy at least twice her size and said, "Bring it on!" Of course, after she said it, she ran in the opposite direction as fast as possible.

I would love to tell you that the girls and I pulled out a huge victory. We didn't even come close. As a matter of fact, I believe those boys scored at least 12 times our score. However, what I am more pleased to tell you is that we all had the most riotous, chaotic, insanely fun 15 minutes that even now, I have to laugh when I think about it. My children, from the time the lights dimmed until the final bell rang, were like a group of special ops ground troops. They dove behind walls, they tripped and flew around corners and got right back up. My older two formed a unit and waited with their backs against the wall and surprised all five boys at once. I swear to you, my five-year-old dove through a cutout in the wall, did a headfirst forward roll, landed in a crouch position, got one of them in the back, and blew into the top of her laser shooter.

If I had been armed with a video camera that day, I think we would have less trouble in this house figuring out what we all want to watch. And I think those teenage boys, if only out of sheer amusement had a great time too. And now we have a memory…a wonderful, hysterical memory.

* * *

Over the course of the afternoon, looking at the photo album, we turned page after page of memorable events in our lives.

We recalled the birthday party where we had rearranged our home into a temporary carnival, complete with strings of flashing lights, about ten booth games, and an iron-on T-shirt "store." We found pictures of beloved pets that had passed on. Pictures of holidays gone by and school plays attended. Of fishing and swimming. Of gymnastics and cheerleading. Many memories…all with a wonderful nostalgia attached to them.

It's funny about the pictures that never make it into a photo album. The events that sometimes carry more significance than anything you could capture on film. Like the first time your child falls down and skins her knee. You simply don't rush off and get your camera when this happens, and ask the child to hold still so Mommy can get a clear photo of the wound. Instead, you rush over to gather up your toddler, then take her inside to bandage the wound. Or the time your daughter doesn't get the solo spot in the school play, and comes home crying. You don't ask her to wait until you can capture her raw emotion for the photo album. You take her in your arms and comfort her, and make her feel better.

These are also the times I want my children to remember when they're grown. The times when we as a family were there for each other. The times we all hugged one another and said it would be okay. The times we fought with each other, but always made up. Our daily lives together, helping each other through, one day at a time. I hope my children's memories incorporate those things as well, and when they look back into the photo albums of their minds, I hope they will smile, and remember what it means to be part of a family…whether the family memory is captured, processed, printed or not.

Myth:
I Wouldn't Trade Them for Anything in the World

Chapter twenty-one

Lost Child

The other day my 13-year-old was chatting with her friends on the computer. She had been on the computer for at least three hours, completely uninterrupted. I even put her lunch on a stool next to her so she wouldn't have to physically get up. I, on the other hand, had spent the last 180 minutes washing dishes, fixing a kite, mixing an experimental concoction that is now baking in my oven, and folding the laundry. It is at this point when I make the dreaded mistake of asking my 13-year-old to actually move.

"Honey, your laundry needs to be put away."

No answer.

"Honey, I'm asking you to please take your laundry up and put it away."

She glances in my direction, gives me a look that seems to say I've just cut off her right arm and replies, "Now?"

"Yes, now. I'm going to vacuum and I need these piles off the living room rug."

"Can't you vacuum around them?"

Now I'm the one thoroughly annoyed, so I say in a more forceful tone of voice, "I want you get up, walk over here, and take this laundry without one more word, okay?"

She proceeds to hoist herself from the computer chair in the most dramatic fashion she can, walk over to me with a stride that if I didn't know better, suggests she needs a walker, then huffs as she grabs the miniscule pile of clothing from my arms. It takes her half a minute to cross the room to the stairs, and another two minutes to slowly climb all eleven steps and crawl down the hallway to her room.

At this point the computer makes a dinging noise, signaling that one of her friends has sent her a message. Since the volume on the computer is turned up too high, combined with the supersonic hearing my daughter has suddenly developed, she comes tearing down the stairs, and makes it back to the screen in under five seconds. I want to point out the irony of the situation to her, but having long ago realized that irony is lost on children, I decide to keep quiet.

Later this particular day...I have (God forbid) asked her to put her lunch dish in the sink, and go upstairs to turn off her radio that she left blaring. After the two small tasks, she throws herself on the sofa and exclaims to anyone who will sympathize, how tired she is. I want to laugh, but instead I try to be sympathetic and tell her that maybe she should rest a while. Goodness knows how exhausting the clicking of that little mouse can be.

So this is the way she spends her afternoon: lying on the sofa watching TV, resting. When the phone rings and it's for her, she asks me if I can hand her the portable phone. When I pass her with my arms full of laundry, she asks me if I can grab her a drink, on my way back. When I eventually vacuum the floor, she reaches for the remote like she's crippled, wrinkles her brow, and switches the captions on.

The rest of the day proceeds in the same fashion, and after serving her dinner to her on the coffee table, I check her head to see if she's warm. I tell my husband that she might be coming down with something.

As I am washing the dinner dishes, and planning on scrubbing the kitchen floor, the doorbell rings. I assume that since there are several other capable bodies in the house, and since I am the only body that seems to be engaged in any activity, that someone will answer the door.

However, after three rings, and a "isn't someone going to get that?" I sigh and open the door. There stand two of my thirteen-year-old's friends, who ask if my daughter is home. I am just about to tell them that she is, but she's not feeling well, when the door swings out from behind me, and my daughter says, "I got it, Mom."

I walk back to the kitchen, assuming she is telling her friend how tired she is, and that she can't come out right now. Boy, am I wrong. But this is something I'm getting used to.

"Mom, can I go to the pool with Tracey and Alexa?"

"What, tonight?"

"Yeah. They're walking over there now. Can I go with them?"

"Honey, the pool is a two-mile walk. I thought you weren't feeling well...."

"What made you think that? I never said I was sick."

"But you spent most of the day lying down. You couldn't even get your own drink. Do you remember two hours ago when you said you couldn't get the mail because your legs hurt?"

My daughter proceeds to roll her eyes and head, and informs me that she feels fine now.

I say that she can go, mostly because I am still baffled, and what I see next blows my mind. If I had been carrying a stopwatch, I am certain my daughter would have qualified for the Olympics. Before I can turn around, the child is dressed in her bathing suit, has applied makeup, grabbed a towel, found her ever-elusive shoes, and run out the door yelling "bye!"

I only have time to yell, "Be home by eight!" before she disappears with her friends around our corner.

My husband comes back from the store a few moments later and asks me where the sick child is.

"Not sick."

"No?"

"Just lazy."

"Alright, where's the lazy child then?"

"Running two miles to the pool, to swim, dive and chat all evening, and then running two miles home."

We both decide to avoid coming up with an explanation, and let it go. Over the years, letting perplexing situations go has kept us mostly sane.

At eight, my daughter strolls up to the house, hugs her two friends goodbye, tells them to call her tomorrow, waves violently from the doorway, and then closes the door.

"Did you have fun at the pool?"

No answer. Just a sigh as she hurls her body on the sofa.

"Is something wrong?"

"No, I'm just exhausted. Are you going to the kitchen, because I'm really thirsty."

*   *   *

A while ago a friend of mine found a stray dog. She came to me to ask for help in writing up and printing a lost dog sign since her computer was on the fritz. It got me thinking about how people describe lost pets in order for their owners to recognize them. It made me think of how I could depict my daughter on such a sign (remember, I think too much). I actually got as far as drawing up a rough draft. Tentatively, the sign reads:

•Lost Child——looks to be in her early teens
•Responds to name——sometimes
•Has selective mononucleosis, however, can run miraculously rapidly when responding to things that ring, beep, or invite her out
•Can not sit up or shake yet, however she begs and plays dead quite well
•Doesn't like a leash, but keeps herself groomed nicely
•Has been known to nip and growl on occasion, but overall would make a good child for a very patient family

The other day I teased her about posting this sign on the front door (right next to the lost clothes sign).

"Maybe we'll get a taker?"

My daughter gave me that squinty-eyed look that says, "very funny mom."

A few days later, I found a piece of paper lying on the pillow in my bedroom. I picked it up and read:

•Lost Mother——not quite sure of age, looks old
•Responds to loud bangs and the sound of glass breaking

•Has selective schizophrenia when she sees something that's not cleaned up
•Can not roll over very well and is slow to learn new tricks, however, makes a great watchdog
•Doesn't like to play fetch, but keeps our house groomed nicely
•Has been known to bark and yelp, but overall would make a good mom for a very patient family

After reading my daughter's "Mother" sign, I decided to addend the "Lost Daughter" sign and attach the following:

•Good sense of humor
•Wouldn't trade her for a million dollars

My daughter in turn added to the "Lost Mom" sign:

•Good sense of humor
•Will negotiate

At this juncture, the million dollars isn't looking too bad…

Myth:
They Will Take Root Quickly and Be Ever Strong

Chapter twenty-two

The Tree of Uncertainty

We moved into our house seven years ago in the spring. I distinctly remember when we first pulled into the driveway to look at our future home. There was a beautiful tree in the front yard. It had large pink and white flowers on every branch, and was in its full and glorious springtime bloom. That spring was the last time I was to ever see this tree in its entire splendor. I have no idea what occurred over the course of the years after we moved in, but our tree never looked the same.

I secretly supposed that the previous owner poured a truckload of Miracle Grow on the thing before running off and leaving us at the tree's mercy. Since that day we have discovered that we are the proud owners of a magnolia tree, and because I don't buy any flowering plants that don't contain "hearty" in the small tag description, we were already in trouble. Apparently magnolias thrive in the south, where the weather stays warmer longer. We of course do not live in the south, which should have been the first indication there was to be difficulty.

Now our family can't claim total immunity when it comes to the growth and development of the tree. I mean there was the year when the girls picked most of the fuzzies off the lower half to make mud soup (supposedly fuzzies are an essential ingredient). None of us bothered to think that those fuzzies were actually pods with buds in them. There was also the time when my youngest took up a stint of tree-climbing and broke a branch off the left side, rendering the tree lopsided for two seasons. But not all tree mishaps were of our doing. Mother Nature played a role as well.

Three falls ago the tree was on the edge of blooming and I made all the children come out to observe.

"Tomorrow, girls, this tree should actually look like it should! Isn't that exciting?"

"Yeah, mom, that's great..."

That night the first frost came, and all the buds opened black. Completely shriveled and black.

But this tree, while frustrating, and disappointing, and sometimes just downright ugly, got me thinking about life, and how really confusing it is. Our tree never asked to be placed in a northern climate. It never wanted to be picked at, and broken, and frosted on. It probably had a whole different existence planned out for itself.

Well, first I'll grow up in Florida, and then when I'm old enough to bud I'll be the prettiest tree around. Every year people will just stop and stare at my loveliness. Maybe I'll even be planted in a park somewhere way up on a hill, so everyone for miles will see my splendor....

Well, little tree, welcome to northern Pennsylvania. Welcome to a place where at any moment in September you could be barraged with cold winds and frost. Where just when you are about to try to bloom for yet another year, young children come and pick off your buds. Where you could lose a branch to a tree-climbing hooligan at any time. Where an Indian Summer in late September gives you new hope that you may indeed bloom, that this could be your year, only to have your flowers open up shriveled and black.

That's kind of like how life is. You start off young and eager, thinking all circumstances are up to you, that you make your own destiny, and then you get planted somewhere else. But you try and make the best of it, and start dreaming of the flowers that you'll someday have. And then a frost comes, and you bloom tired and stunted. Or someone happens by and breaks off your branches or plucks off your pods of hope.

If I were our tree, I would've uprooted a long time ago. I would have moved somewhere where people wouldn't break me, or the surroundings weren't so harsh. At the very least I would've started swatting young children every time they tried to steal the fruits of my labor....

Or would I? Would I really run from troubles or people who insist on taking from me? The more I think about it, the more I am convinced that my tree, my misplaced magnolia tree, has it right. Through all the hardships and the trials, it stands firm. It does not surrender, whither and die. Instead every year it tries to grow a new crop of hope. It tries to make a new start.

I am happy to report, that this spring our magnolia tree bloomed. Not all of it mind you, but enough to see that possibly next year or the year after that, it could look like the year we first moved in. I summoned my whole family out on the front lawn to witness the miracle of the tree. I even shed a few tears. My oldest daughter rolled her eyes at me, and told me that I needed a life.

"Just wait until you're a tree, and you fight hard to bloom! Then you'll understand!" I called after her.

Of course she is already on the hard path of growing up, and unlike our tree, she will have a great many more choices as to where she plants her roots, and who she holds close to her branches.

I simply hope she will learn to fight through cold winters, abide unexpected damage and re-grow optimistic shoots after some cruel individual or unfair incident injures the heart of her tree.

I hope she fights to always remember spring is coming.

I hope someday she too will bloom.

Acknowledgments

First and foremost, to my Lord and Savior Jesus Christ, my greatest thanks for allowing me to even wake up each morning, much less giving me this opportunity to live out a dream.

To David, my other half, all my love and thanks for believing in me. Without you this book would've never been written.

To James and Sandra Cottrell and family, without whom my family would most certainly be living in a cardboard box, I can't thank you enough for all your compassion and generosity over the years.

To my mom Ruth, my sisters Patty and Debbie, my brother-in-law Ed, my adopted father Ed, and all the rest of my family, all my love. Thanks for all the encouragement along my writing journey.

To my partner in literary crime, Lori, thanks for all of your support.

To my friend Cindy, thanks for sharing so many memories with me along the journey.

To Walter, a big thanks for all the hard work put into making this book become a reality.

And to my three beautiful daughters, Erin, Sara and Rachel, without whom I would have no inspiration in the first place... I love you all.